Palgrave Studies in Presidential Politics

Series Editors
Robert Elgie
School of Law & Government
Dublin City University
Dublin, Ireland

Gianluca Passarelli
Sapienza University of Rome
Rome, Italy

Palgrave Studies in Presidential Politics publishes books on all aspects of presidential politics. We welcome proposals for monographs, edited volumes and Pivots on topics such as:

- Contemporary presidencies and presidential powers
- Presidential elections and presidential party politics
- Presidential relations with the legislature
- The media and presidential communication
- The administrative presidency and presidential advisers
- The history of presidential offices and presidential biographies

The series focuses on presidents throughout the world, including both directly elected and indirectly elected presidents, both single-country and comparative studies of presidential politics. It also includes volumes on conceptual or theoretical aspects, such as how to measure presidential power. Moreover, the series considers book projects on the reform of presidential politics, e.g. the reform of presidential elections.

For further information on the series and to submit a proposal for consideration, please get in touch with Commissioning Editor Ambra Finotello **ambra.finotello@palgrave.com**, Series Editors Robert Elgie **robert.elgie@dcu.ie**, and Gianluca Passarelli **gianluca.passarelli@uniroma1.it**.

More information about this series at
http://www.palgrave.com/gp/series/15600

Tapio Raunio • Thomas Sedelius

Semi-Presidential Policy-Making in Europe

Executive Coordination and Political Leadership

Tapio Raunio
Faculty of Management and Business
Tampere University
Tampere, Finland

Thomas Sedelius
School of Education, Health and
Social Sciences
Dalarna University
Falun, Sweden

Palgrave Studies in Presidential Politics
ISBN 978-3-030-16430-0   ISBN 978-3-030-16431-7   (eBook)
https://doi.org/10.1007/978-3-030-16431-7

This Palgrave Macmillan imprint is published by the registered company Springer Nature Switzerland AG
The registered company address is: Gewerbestrasse 11, 6330 Cham, Switzerland

PREFACE

With this book, we conclude a four-year project (2015–2018) about semi-presidentialism in transitional regimes. The overall purpose of this broader project was to provide new theoretical and empirical knowledge on the implications of semi-presidentialism in transitional regimes. We have examined to what extent and in what ways the institutional interaction between the president, prime minister, and parliament matters to governability in semi-presidential regimes. The project has produced large-N studies on democracy and government performance (Sedelius and Linde 2018), diffusion and choice of constitutional regimes (Åberg 2017), and a number of focused comparisons and single-case studies on inter-institutional relations in semi-presidential regimes in Central and Eastern Europe (Raunio and Sedelius 2017; Sedelius 2015, 2016; Sedelius and Åberg 2018).[1]

In terms of conceptual and theoretical framing and level of empirical ambition, research on semi-presidentialism has made significant strides forward during the past two decades. Yet, in a meta-analysis of this sub-field, Åberg and Sedelius (2018) identified a number of important gaps. Among these, they call for more research on political leadership and elites, public administration, informal avenues of influence, and studies that explore the challenges involved in distinguishing between domestic and foreign policies in the context of semi-presidential regimes. The objective of our book is to at least offer exploratory insights about these topics and to encourage further research on intra-executive coordination mechanisms and on presidential strategies and behavior.

This comparative study focuses on actual power-sharing and institutional coordination between the president and the prime minister. Anchored in the new institutionalist tradition, and by no means ignoring formal constitutional rules, party-political dynamics, or the broader societal context, our core idea is to reach further into the halls of executive power-sharing. We are especially interested in the level of institutional coordination at the point where the two executives need to interact directly or indirectly to reach policy goals. In contrast to much of existing comparative work on semi-presidentialism, we emphasize the role of institutions at the most concrete level of executive policy-making. In order to reach 'behind the scenes' and to go beyond most obvious data on political and institutional conditions, we draw mainly on a set of unique expert interview data in Finland, Lithuania, and Romania. Theoretically, we develop a tentative framework based on four strands of literature: semi-presidentialism, public administration, political leadership, and foreign policy analysis. To policy-makers and other stakeholders that might take an interest, we hope that our study will contribute to an increased understanding about effective leadership and policy coordination in semi-presidential regimes.

Tampere, Finland   Tapio Raunio

Falun, Sweden   Thomas Sedelius

NOTE

1. The references are found in the bibliography section of Chap. 1.

ACKNOWLEDGMENTS

The Swedish Research Council under the granted project VR 2014-1260 provided resources to make this book possible. The support of many others, however, was fundamental to get it all done. Conducting expert interviews in three different countries certainly requires a lot of support. We are especially indebted to Bogdan Dima at the Faculty of Law, University of Bucharest, and his assistant, Dragos Petrescu, for coordinating, undertaking, and translating the interviews in Romania, and similarly to Sigita Trainauskiene at the Research and Higher Education Monitoring Research Center in Vilnius, who did the corresponding work in Lithuania. We certainly appreciate all the time you have put into this project.

Our sincerest gratitude goes to each one of the 30 anonymous experts in Finland, Lithuania, and Romania, who agreed to be interviewed and who shared so much of their unique expertise from the inside of their political systems. Due to the sensitive nature of the interview topics, they are unnamed in this book but include current and former high-level civil servants, counselors, and advisors in the offices of the president and the prime minister, speakers and members of parliament, and ministers, including one former prime minister.

We are also grateful to our colleagues and friends in the political science department at Dalarna University, who gave valuable remarks and comments on chapter drafts and early papers of this book project. Especially, we should mention Jenny Åberg, Kjetil Duvold, Ulf Hansson, Erik Lundberg, Jenny Lönnemyr, and Mats Öhlén. During the writing of the book, we have called upon colleagues with expertise on Lithuania and Romania to comment on certain sections and chapter drafts. Algis

Krupavičius, Bogdan Dima, and especially Veronica Anghel deserve our warm gratitude in this regard. Needless to say, remaining errors and misinterpretations rest entirely with us.

Our project has also benefited substantially from feedback by colleagues at various conferences—especially the Presidential Politics Sections at the European Consortium of Political Research (ECPR) General Conferences in Oslo 2017 and Hamburg 2018. This includes, among others, Carsten Anckar, Miloš Brunclík, Cristina Bucur, Martin Carrier, Svitlana Chernykh, Robert Elgie, Rui Graça Feijó, Vít Hloušek, Michal Kubát, Philipp Köker, Sébastien Lazardeux, Sophia Moestrup, Malkhaz Nakashidze, Gianluca Passarelli, Timothy Power, and Joseph Tsai.

Finally, we would like to thank the Palgrave editors Ambra Finotello and Anne-Kathrin Birchley-Brun for guiding us through the processing of this book, and Robert Elgie and Gianluca Passarelli, series editors of *Palgrave Studies in Presidential Politics*, as well as the anonymous reviewer, for being constructive and supportive of the project.

Faculty of Management and Business,   Tapio Raunio
Tampere University, Tampere, Finland
January 2019
School of Education, Health and Social Sciences,   Thomas Sedelius
Dalarna University, Falun, Sweden

CONTENTS

1 Introduction 1
   1.1 Aim and Research Questions 2
   1.2 What Is Semi-Presidentialism and What Do We Know About It? 3
   1.3 Why Study Executive Coordination in Semi-Presidential Regimes? 6
   1.4 Research Design and Data 7
   1.5 Outline of the Book 12
   Appendix 13
   Bibliography 14

2 Institutions, Coordination, and Leadership 19
   2.1 Institutional Theory and Policy Coordination 20
   2.2 Semi-Presidentialism and the Challenge of Cooperation 25
   2.3 Foreign Policy and the Challenge of Leadership 30
   2.4 Theoretical Framework and Coordination Mechanisms 34
   Bibliography 41

3 The Semi-Presidential Cases in Comparative Context 45
   3.1 Semi-Presidential Regimes in Europe 45
   3.2 Presidential Power 52
   3.3 President-Cabinet Conflict and Cohabitation 58

3.4 Public Trust in the President and Other Institutions   66
3.5 A Comparative Design with Explorative Ambitions   72
Bibliography   74

4 Formal Coordination Mechanisms   79
4.1 Establishing Variation Between Finland, Lithuania,
     and Romania   80
4.2 Explaining the Variation   87
Bibliography   90

5 Informal Avenues of Influence   93
5.1 Finland: Constrained Presidency   94
5.2 Lithuania: Presidents Stamping Their Authority   99
5.3 Romania: When Mediation Goes Too Far   108
5.4 Concluding Discussion: 'where is it forbidden?'   119
Bibliography   124

6 Decision-Making in Foreign and Security Policies and EU
   Affairs   127
6.1 Finland: Establishing a Logical Division of Labor   128
6.2 Lithuania: Presidential 'Power Grabs'   135
6.3 Romania: President as the Undisputed Leader in Foreign
     Affairs   141
6.4 Concluding Reflections: Consensus but Potential for
     Disputes   145
Bibliography   149

7 Conclusions   151
7.1 Informal Avenues and Political Leadership   152
7.2 Popular and Dangerous Presidents?   160

Index   165

LIST OF FIGURES

Fig. 2.1   Theoretical framework: executive coordination and
           presidential activism   35
Fig. 2.2   Institutions of executive coordination: a tentative model   37
Fig. 3.1   Public evaluation of the powers of the president in Finland
           1990–2017, percentages   69
Fig. 3.2   Public evaluation of the powers of the parliament in Finland
           1990–2017, percentages   69
Fig. 3.3   Public opinion on presidential power in Finland 2018,
           percentages   70

LIST OF TABLES

Table 3.1   Comparative indicators on semi-presidential countries in
             Europe   46
Table 3.2   Nations in Transit 2010–2018, ratings and average scores:
             Lithuania and Romania   51
Table 3.3   Doyle and Elgie's presidential power scores in European
             semi-presidential countries   53
Table 3.4   Shugart and Carey's presidential power scores in European
             semi-presidential countries   54
Table 3.5   Siaroff's presidential power scores in European semi-
             presidential countries   55
Table 3.6   Presidential power scores, Finland 1919–2018   57
Table 3.7   Intra-executive conflict and presidential power: Elgie
             (2018a) and Sedelius and Mashtaler (2013) scores   59
Table 3.8   Intra-executive conflict and periods of cohabitation   61
Table 3.9   Trust in institutions 2001–2014, Estonia, Latvia, Lithuania
             (percentages)   67
Table 3.10   Trust in institutions 2001–2016, Czech Republic, Poland,
             Romania (percentages)   67
Table 4.1   Intra-executive coordination mechanisms in Finland,
             Lithuania, and Romania   81
Table 7.1   Summary of main findings   154

CHAPTER 1

Introduction

Research on semi-presidentialism has emerged into a burgeoning subfield, with comparisons between regime types followed by comparisons between various types of semi-presidential countries (Elgie 2016; Åberg and Sedelius 2018). However, much of this research is theoretically and conceptually quite narrow. Studies have focused on regime stability, with authors interested in how variables such as presidential power or divided government affect the level of conflict between the two executives (Beuman 2016; Elgie 2018a). Some semi-presidential countries are more heavily affected by conflict than others, and certain periods within the same countries are more conflictive than others. Yet in most cases a dual executive seems to work without stalemate or instability (Elgie and McMenamin 2011). Another important line of inquiry has compared regime types, examining how semi-presidentialism is linked to various macro-political outcomes such as democratic performance and survival (e.g. Cheibub et al. 2014; Elgie 2011; Hicken and Stoll 2013; Sedelius and Linde 2018).

However, despite more than two decades of research on semi-presidential dynamics, we still know very little about the actual functioning of day-to-day routines and coordination between the president and the prime minister and about the various channels through which presidents wield influence. Executive policy coordination in semi-presidential regimes remains something of a blind spot in the current literature. To be sure, country studies have detailed relational dynamics between the president and the prime minister (e.g. Gherghina and Miscoiu 2013;

© The Author(s) 2020
T. Raunio, T. Sedelius, *Semi-Presidential Policy-Making in Europe*,
Palgrave Studies in Presidential Politics,
https://doi.org/10.1007/978-3-030-16431-7_1

Lazardeux 2015; Raunio 2012; Shen 2011; Shoesmith 2003), but without developing a systematic and comparative understanding of executive coordination in semi-presidential regimes. These studies do suggest that there is considerable variation between semi-presidential countries in how actual policy coordination and power-sharing mechanisms operate and to what extent such mechanisms are codified into constitutional rules. To our knowledge, there are no studies identifying operative mechanisms inside the semi-presidential system, such as bilateral meetings between the president and the cabinet, the organization and operation of committees and councils, or the administrative and expert resources available to the president and the cabinet, and how these are related to presidential activism. This book wants to contribute both theoretically and empirically on such key institutional aspects of semi-presidentialism.

1.1   Aim and Research Questions

The aim of this study is to dig deeper—beyond constitutional rules—into the mechanisms of executive coordination and policy-making in semi-presidential regimes. Based on a focused comparative design including unique expert interview data from two Central European countries, Lithuania and Romania, and one long-lasting case of European semi-presidentialism, Finland, we ask how coordination between the president and the prime minister actually works and how it influences the balance of power within the executive. We raise three main research questions guiding our endeavor:

1. Across our three selected cases of semi-presidentialism, to what extent is coordination between the president and the prime minister established by formal institutional mechanisms such as codified rules and/or organizational bodies?
2. In what ways do variations on the level of institutional coordination between the president and the prime minister matter to presidential activism and executive power-sharing?
3. In addition to what previous research teaches us about intra-executive conflict and power-sharing in semi-presidential regimes, how may scholarly work on executive coordination help to further advance the study of semi-presidentialism?

As for our theoretical contribution, we build on different strands of literature (semi-presidentialism, public administration, political leadership, and foreign policy analysis) to develop an analytical framework subsequently applied on the three selected country cases. Given the political challenges facing many semi-presidential countries, the study also seeks to identify institutional solutions that facilitate power-sharing and successful policy-making.

1.2   What Is Semi-Presidentialism and What Do We Know About It?

Defining semi-presidentialism has proved to be far more complicated than defining parliamentarism and presidentialism. Parliamentarism has an authority structure based on mutual dependence between the parliament and the government, whereas presidentialism is defined by separation of powers where a popularly elected president names and directs the composition of government, and is not contingent on mutual confidence. Semi-presidential regimes, on the other hand, have dual elections (presidential and legislative), but the survival of the prime minister and the government is dependent on the maintenance of parliamentary support.

Since Duverger's founding definition[1] of semi-presidentialism, there has been an enduring discussion on how to define and categorize regimes with a dual executive, including both a popularly elected president and a prime minister. Duverger's (1980: 4) non-institutional criterion that "the president possesses quite considerable powers" has caused debate and confusion. Scholars have approached it differently and the classification of semi-presidential countries has varied extensively.

In the 2000s, comparative scholars began to increasingly accept the use of strictly constitutional definitions. Robert Elgie partly resolved the matter when proposing a minimalist definition, stating that "semi-presidentialism is where a constitution includes a popularly elected fixed-term president and a prime minister and cabinet who are collectively responsible to the legislature" (Elgie 1999: 13). Elgie's definition has attracted considerable critique for encompassing too many and disparate countries, however. Elgie has acknowledged that his definition is mainly taxonomic and recommended that it should not be used as a discrete variable for explanatory purposes (Elgie and Moestrup 2016: 9–11). For both theoretical and empirical reasons, we need to separate between different forms of semi-presidentialism. Among alternatives in the literature, Shugart and Carey's subcategorization of premier-presidential and president-parliamentary regimes has received broad acceptance. Premier-presidentialism is where (1) the president is elected by a popular vote for a fixed term in office; (2) the president selects the prime minister, who heads the cabinet; but (3) the authority to dismiss the cabinet rests exclusively with the parliament. President-parliamentarism is where (1) the president is elected by a popular vote for a fixed term in office, (2) the president appoints and dismisses the prime minister and other cabinet ministers, and (3) the prime minister and cabinet ministers are subjected to parliamentary as well as to presidential confidence (Shugart and Carey 1992: 23–24; Shugart 2005: 333). The key difference is that under president-parliamentarism the government is accountable to both the president and the parliament, whereas under premier-presidentialism the government is accountable only to the parliament. In addition, president-parliamentary constitutions do usually provide overall stronger presidential prerogatives.

The fall of the Soviet Union in 1991, and the emergence of many new semi-presidential countries during the 1990s, marked the start of an increasing research focus on semi-presidentialism. Research has seen differing definitions, varying country samples, and shifting research topics. Yet the field has evolved from a set of ideas anchored in Linz's argument for parliamentarism and against presidentialism. Scholars have addressed the assumed perils associated with semi-presidential constitutions and the findings have both challenged and supported these claims. Generally, the literature gives little or no support in favor of president-parliamentarism (Shugart and Carey 1992; Elgie 2011; Elgie and Moestrup 2016; Sedelius and Linde 2018) and reveals more mixed or positive performance records regarding premier-presidentialism (Elgie 2011; Moestrup 2007; Samuels and Shugart 2010; Sedelius and Linde 2018). In this study, we focus exclusively on premier-presidential countries and only on European democracies that are also member states of the European Union (EU).

Schleiter and Morgan-Jones (2009: 891) argue that the last decade has seen "a rapid broadening of the research agenda beyond Linz's concern with the adverse effects of presidents on democratic stability". To what extent the field has actually moved on from Linz's proposition about the perils of (semi-) presidentialism is debatable, but the research agenda has gradually shifted from grand questions about expected regime effects toward the institutional operation of semi-presidentialism. Of particular relevance in regard to our study, there has been an increased focus on the relation between the key institutional actors. In addition to studies on the role of the president and the party system (Passarelli 2015; Samuels and Shugart 2010), research on intra-executive relations between the president and the prime minister has become more common (Amorim Neto and Costa Lobo 2009; Carrier 2015; Elgie 2018a; Protsyk 2005, 2006).

In premier-presidential systems, the legislature enjoys exclusive power to dismiss the prime minister. The government is thus likely to reflect the parliamentary majority's policy orientation rather than that of the president. On theoretical grounds, therefore, intra-executive conflicts are to be expected. Empirical findings seem to confirm this expectation, as well as suggesting that the likelihood of intra-executive conflict and the prospects for forming a government reflect the extent of presidential powers, the party structure of the parliament, and even the presidential ambitions of the prime minister (Amorim Neto and Strøm 2006; Protsyk 2005, 2006; Schleiter and Morgan-Jones 2010). Sedelius and Ekman's (2010) study on intra-executive conflict in Eastern Europe suggests that such conflicts are associated with pre-term resignation of governments.

Intra-executive conflict may result from cohabitation, that is, "where the president and prime minister are from opposing parties and where the president's party is not represented in cabinet" (Elgie 2011: 12). Cohabitation may cause tension and undermine general performance, especially when the democracy in question is young, or when there is no clear-cut constitutional provision setting out the distribution of power among the key actors (Elgie 2010; Gherghina and Miscoiu 2013; Shoesmith 2003; Skach 2005). Non-concurrent elections and a presidency with weak power seem to make cohabitation more likely (Shugart and Carey 1992; Samuels and Shugart 2010). However, cohabitation seems to be a situation that arises in contexts where it can be managed within democratic bounds and without threatening democratic stability (Elgie 2010).

Principal-agent theory has contributed substantially to our knowledge of the operation and challenges of semi-presidential regimes. However, the principal-agent approach is limited to the extent that it tends to treat institutions as static entities, focusing mainly on the causal direction from institutions to actors and not the other way around (Peters 2012). In this study, we recognize the need to add other strains of New Institutionalism to intra-executive relations in order to emphasize the importance of factors such as past institutional experiences and path dependency. Historical-institutional analysis helps to improve our understanding of the way that context influences actor preferences. In addition, Normative Institutionalism emphasizes patterns of institutional change and portrays institutional choice as reflecting norms and notions of legitimacy held by the actors involved. By anchoring our study in a broader set of new institutional approaches, combined with assumptions derived from the literature on political leadership and foreign policy analysis, we strive to offer a tailored framework for analyzing executive coordination in semi-presidential regimes.

1.3   Why Study Executive Coordination in Semi-Presidential Regimes?

Through new in-depth data, we consider the importance of factors that are largely overlooked in the current literature, such as the size and resources of the presidential administration, the operation of executive committees and other intra-executive coordination bodies, and the inherent norms and expectations concerning the power and role of the president among the political and administrative elites. Our book makes four main contributions to the literature on semi-presidentialism and policy-making.

1. *A multidisciplinary theoretical approach.* Drawing on four strands of literature that are rarely combined—semi-presidentialism, public administration, political leadership, and foreign policy analysis—our theoretical approach underscores the importance of institutions in facilitating successful leadership and policy coordination. Hence we ask 'do institutions matter' at the level of normal intra-executive decision-making. Our basic premise is that institutional design is related to the level of conflict between the cabinet and the president, and that conflict over policy, legislation, or appointments are manifestations of coordination problems. By institutional design, we mean those rules, organizational arrangements, and conventions that structure routine coordination between the two executives.
2. *An in-depth analysis of intra-executive decision-making.* We examine three countries: Finland, Lithuania, and Romania. Drawing on in-depth expert interviews with top-level civil servants and politicians (including cabinet ministers), official documents, and complementary material such as biographies, we dig deeper—beyond constitutional rules and divided government—to explore the operational level of semi-presidential decision-making. Using secondary material, the three countries are also compared with other semi-presidential regimes.

3. *Uncovering foreign policy leadership.* Directly elected European presidents normally have at least some role in the external relations of their countries. Foreign and security policy is for most countries a very sensitive and important domain. It is also a policy area where unified and clear leadership is valued and where disunity at home should not undermine success abroad. Hence, in semi-presidential regimes, intra-executive conflicts are viewed as particularly detrimental in foreign relations. Moreover, the foreign policies of EU member states are increasingly linked to decision-making at the European level. In most semi-presidential regimes, EU policy belongs to the jurisdiction of the government, but presidents may be involved, not least in foreign and security matters and through their right to veto or delay the domestic ratification of Treaty amendments. This raises important questions about intra-executive coordination and representation at the European level. Benefiting from access to people directly involved in the planning and implementation of foreign and security policies, we examine how leadership in foreign and EU policies works in the three semi-presidential regimes.

4. *Identification of conditions facilitating successful policy-making.* The study of semi-presidentialism has been understandably preoccupied with intra-executive conflict and regime stability. This conflict potential is exacerbated in new democracies, where the distribution of authority is often more ambiguous and fluid. Our combination of in-depth case knowledge and comparative approach enables us to identify factors that contribute to coherent decision-making. We emphasize the role of institutions—both the legal framework and organizational arrangements—without neglecting other variables such as party system dynamics or the broader political culture.

1.4   Research Design and Data

Based on a most-similar comparative case study design including on the one hand two Central European countries—Lithuania and Romania, and on the other hand Finland as a long-lasting case of European semi-presidentialism, we make comparisons within as well as between the countries. In Chap. 3, we will set these countries in a wider comparative context of semi-presidentialism in Europe to justify more carefully the selection of cases for the focused comparison that follows in Chaps. 4, 5 and 6. At this point, however, we will just briefly introduce the idea behind our case selection. After that we shall introduce our data.

The selection is based on the logic of similarities. Finland aside, there is the shared legacy of systemic communism in Lithuania and Romania, their subsequent transition to democracy and market economy in the 1990s, and the EU and the North Atlantic Treaty Organization (NATO) accession processes in the 2000s. However, the selection of cases is also based on the fact that they embody different patterns of intra-executive dynamics. Each country represents a unique semi-presidential path: high levels of institutionalization and the weakening of a historically strong presidency in Finland in 2000; general intra-executive stability under a personalized political system in Lithuania; and party system instability, strong presidential influence, personalized politics, and high institutional tensions in Romania.

Finland Until the 1980s, Finland's semi-presidential system was characterized by powerful presidents with a strong executive role in managing the country's sensitive relations with the Soviet Union. For the last three decades, however, there has been a gradual marginalization of the president's position in the political system. Finland adopted a new constitution in 2000, which formally restricted the executive role of the president. Since then, the Finnish president has very limited authority in government formation and dissolution matters, decision-making, decree issues, as well as in vetoing legislative bills. Finland is thus a case of a constitutionally weak presidency embedded in an institutional legacy of strong presidential figures. We are interested in the extent to which such institutional legacies impact on the coordination and policy-making between the president and the government. In addition, Finland's long-term experience of enduring democracy under a highly institutionalized political system is comparatively attractive when analyzing the newer experiences of semi-presidentialism in Central Europe.

Lithuania Previous analyses of semi-presidentialism in Eastern and Central Europe suggest that Lithuania is among the countries with the lowest frequency of intra-executive conflict (Protsyk 2006; Sedelius and Mashtaler 2013), which makes it a particularly interesting case for our study. Quite normal for semi-presidential regimes, the relations between the president and the government have shifted quite significantly during the post-Soviet period and despite the relative stability of the Lithuanian political system, scholars have characterized it as personality-centered (Duvold and Jurkynas 2004). Personality-centered politics does create favorable conditions for presidential activism, which we expect to see reflected in policy coordination and power-sharing between the president and the government.

Romania Among our three cases, Romania has faced the most severe transitional difficulties and is yet struggling with ineffective policy-making, widespread corruption, and recurring political crises. The turbulent and violent transition from communism implicated intra-executive relations early on. There was for instance an intense conflict culminating in violent demonstrations between President Iliescu and Prime Minister Roman already in 1991. Although the president's role in policy-making is constitutionally limited, the presidents to date have exercised considerable influence on Romanian politics. Cohabitation in Romania has tended to generate high levels of institutional conflict and has two times (2007 and 2012) ended in impeachment procedures against the president. It is thus interesting to examine whether such disruptive political processes and institutional crises have led to the establishment of alternative institutional mechanisms for managing policy coordination between the executives.

Expert Interviews

We have set out to use case study expertise to add to a more coherent and in-depth understanding of the operation of semi-presidentialism. A number of political experts on each country were contacted in order to collect information on how the semi-presidential systems have worked in practice with regard to executive relations and coordination mechanisms. Having charted the existence of coordination mechanisms, the key objective of the interviews was to establish the actual role and importance of these institutions. Hence the interviewed persons were selected based on either their long-standing experience of intra-executive relations and/or of current practices. Many of them had experience of intra-executive coordination under two or more presidents. The positions of the interviewees include current and former high-level civil servants, counselors, and advisors in the offices of the president and the prime minister, speakers and members of parliaments, and ministers, including one former prime minister.

The interviews followed a semi-structured format with a set of prepared questions (see Appendix) but which allowed the respondents to elaborate quite freely on the covered issue. The topics are obviously quite sensitive and the interviewees were willing to speak only under the condition of anonymity. In total 10 persons were interviewed in Finland, with the interviews taking place ten years apart, in spring 2008 and in spring 2018; 9 persons in Lithuania in the early spring of 2016; and 11 persons in Romania in the spring of 2017. Native academic colleagues working in the targeted countries undertook the interviews in Lithuania and Romania. The authors are indeed highly indebted to Dr. Sigita Trainauskiene at the Research and Higher Education Monitoring Research Center in Vilnius and to Dr. Bogdan Dima and his associate Mr. Dragos Petrescu at the University of Bucharest for their work in Lithuania and Romania. These colleagues helped with suggesting names of experts as well as accessing them at the very outset, and finally interviewing them, with almost all interviews conducted face to face. Since the authors of this study do not master either Lithuanian or Romanian, we have used transcriptions of the interviews translated into English by our colleagues in the respective country. This necessarily means that certain nuances, implicit understanding, and subtexts may have been lost in our final interpretation of the data. Needless to say, any such interpretation errors rest entirely on us. In the case of Finland, on the contrary, we benefited from Raunio's country expertise and from using his extensive network of top-level contacts to undertake the interviews directly in Finnish. Thus, we acknowledge this apparent imbalance in terms of the authors' first-hand access and previous knowledge about Finland on the one hand, and our more limited expertise and language barrier with regard to Lithuania and Romania on the other.

Documents and Literature

The expert interviews are accompanied by a number of written sources, including official documents, academic literature, reports, and secondary material, including biographies of presidents. The official documents mainly consist of the respective constitutions and relevant laws, as well as governments' rules of procedure and similar documents regulating intra-executive coordination. In addition, we use a conventional mix of academic literature (comparative and case study oriented), country-specific reports, and updates, including online resources such as the research-based blog *Presidential Power*, by Robert Elgie and his associates.

Macro-Level Indicators and Measures

For the wider comparative outlook on semi-presidentialism in Europe (Chap. 3), we use a set of available macro-level indicators and system-level data. In addition to standard indicators on basic conditions such as level of democracy, electoral system, and corruption (e.g. *Freedom House* and *Transparency International*), we report on president-cabinet relations including instances of cohabitation and conflict (Elgie 2018a, b; Sedelius and Mashtaler 2013) and various measures of presidential power (Doyle and Elgie 2016; Elgie and Moestrup 2008; Shugart and Carey 1992; Siaroff 2003). For the selected cases, we also report on public surveys tapping trust in the presidency and other institutions, including data on how citizens in Finland perceive the role of the president in relation to various policy areas (*The New Baltic/Europe Barometers* 2001 and 2004, *The Baltic Barometer* 2014, the *Social Political Survey in Central Europe* 2016, and the *EVA Attitude and Value Survey in Finland* 1990–2018).

Our data can be criticized for not being sufficiently systematic—a theme we will return to in the concluding chapter of this book. This applies particularly to various channels or types of presidential activism, such as public speeches, press releases, or the extent to which the president maintains contacts with political parties and civil society stakeholders. Nor do we explore in any great detail the various intra-executive conflicts: these have for the main part been extensively covered in previous research and in online blog texts. Here we must emphasize that we purposefully focus on broader, general patterns of behavior, regarding both forms of intra-executive coordination and presidential activism, in order to uncover both variation between our three cases and over-time developments within individual countries. It is also self-evident that much of intra-executive coordination and presidential activism leaves no public trace, and hence many of the features explored in this book can only be understood through talking to people with first-hand knowledge of what goes on behind the scenes.

1.5   OUTLINE OF THE BOOK

Having introduced our research design and explained how it contributes to scholarly understanding of semi-presidentialism, Chap. 2 explains our theoretical approach. Building on four strands of literature—semi-presidentialism, public administration, political leadership, and foreign policy analysis—we highlight the role of institutions for successful policy-making and the incentives and disincentives for executive coordination. The chapter concludes with a section where we pull together different strands of literature and put forward a theoretical framework for the subsequent empirical analyses.

Chapter 3 presents the basic features of the Finnish, Lithuanian, and Romanian regimes in a wider comparative context of European semi-presidential regimes and provides a more detailed justification for selecting these cases for further analysis. We provide key data on semi-presidential subtypes (premier-presidentialism and president-parliamentarism), level of democracy, presidential power, intra-executive conflict, and cohabitation. We also assess, by the use of public opinion data, levels of public trust with an emphasis on support for the president.

The subsequent three empirical chapters (Chaps. 4, 5 and 6) are comparative and organized thematically. Chapter 4 examines formal coordination mechanisms such as joint meetings between the president and the prime minister, joint councils, and ministerial committees and the status of such instruments of coordination (legal, conventions, ad hoc). We draw a link between the constitutional powers of the presidents and the level of coordination. We present results from the three countries and explore how the mechanisms have evolved over time.

Having investigated the existence of formal coordination devices, Chap. 5 focuses on the actual coordination and decision-making between the president and the prime minister. Our main argument is that lack of written rules or otherwise strong norms guiding intra-executive coordination opens the door for presidential activism, with presidents enjoying more discretion in designing their own modes of operation. Where strong de facto coordination mechanisms exist, presidents are in turn more constrained and constructively involved in decision-making. The analysis includes agenda-setting initiatives, public opinion and party system dynamics, and the way formal prerogatives are interpreted into praxis, as well as how the key actors approach coordination where there is no explicit constitutional or judicial guidance.

Whereas the two previous chapters analyzed overall intra-executive coordination, Chap. 6 zooms in on foreign and security policy and EU affairs, examining decision-making and division of labor between the president and the prime minister. We again highlight the role of institutions, but also show how constitutional rules about jurisdictions tend to bend in favor of presidents. In order to grasp the complexity of intra-executive policy coordination in these areas, the interdependence between foreign and EU policies is in the spotlight of our attention.

Finally, Chap. 7 focuses on the interaction between institutions and other variables in explaining the observed variation and similarities and the 'shifting centers of power' in semi-presidential regimes. It summarizes the main findings, connects them to the theoretical literature introduced in Chap. 2, and draws lessons about successful policy-making as well as policy or coordination failures. We finally put forward suggestions for future research and offer some general thoughts on the conditions for policy-making and power-sharing in semi-presidential systems.

Appendix

Guiding questions used for semi-structured interviews with experts in Finland, Lithuania, and Romania. While this formed the core set of questions for each interviewee, additional questions were also asked depending on the positions held by the interviewed persons.

1. Can you tell us how coordination between the president and the prime minister and/or the government works?
2. Which forms of coordination are most important and why? Has the importance of various coordination mechanisms changed over time?
3. Is there regular coordination at the level of civil servants between the president's office and the prime minister's office? If yes, what forms does this take?
4. The powers of the president cover legislation (veto), appointments, and foreign policy. Are there differences in coordination between these issues?
5. According to the constitution, the president leads foreign policy but implements it together with the government. The government is responsible for EU policy while the president has attended the European Council meetings. How does cooperation in foreign and EU policies work?

6. Both the president and the prime minister give speeches and meet foreign leaders at home and abroad. Is there coordination regarding such activities? For example, are president's speeches checked beforehand by the prime minister's office?
7. If there is disagreement between the president and the prime minister over some issue (legislation, appointments, foreign policy, etc.), what is the main mechanism for attempting to solve the matter?
8. Can you identify a recent issue that would serve as an example of policy coordination between the president and the prime minister?
9. To what extent would you say that the forms of president/cabinet coordination matter to the relationship between the president and the cabinet? Does it affect policy outcomes or other political aspects? In what way?

NOTE

1. Duverger (1980: 4) provided a definition of semi-presidentialism including three criteria: (1) the president is elected by universal suffrage, (2) the president possesses quite considerable powers, and (3) there is also a prime minister and other ministers who possesses executive and governmental power and can stay in office only with the consent of the parliament.

BIBLIOGRAPHY

Åberg, J. (2017). *Imitating the Neighbors? A Multinominal Logistic Regression Analysis of Regime Type Choices as Related to Time and Space.* Paper presented at Method Conference, Lund University.

Åberg, J., & Sedelius, T. (2018). Review Article: A Structured Review of Semi-Presidential Studies: Debates, Results and Missing Pieces. *British Journal of Political Science*, First View. https://doi.org/10.1017/S0007123418000017.

Amorim Neto, O., & Costa Lobo, M. (2009). Portugal's Semi-Presidentialism (Re)considered: An Assessment of the President's Role in the Policy Process, 1976–2006. *European Journal of Political Research, 48*(2), 234–255.

Amorim Neto, O., & Strøm, K. (2006). Breaking the Parliamentary Chain of Delegation: Presidents and Non-partisan Cabinet Members in European Democracies. *British Journal of Political Science, 36*(4), 619–643.

Arvo-ja asennetutkimus/EVA Attitude and Value Survey. (2018). www.eva.fi/eng. Accessed 13 Dec 2018.

Beuman, L. M. (2016). *Political Institutions in East Timor: Semi-Presidentialism and Democratisation*. Abingdon: Routledge.

Carrier, M. (2015). *Executive Politics in Semi-Presidential Regimes: Power Distribution and Conflict Between Presidents and Prime Ministers*. Lanham: Lexington Books.

Cheibub, J. A., Elkins, Z., & Ginsburg, T. (2014). Beyond Presidentialism and Parliamentarism. *British Journal of Political Science, 44*(3), 515–544.

Doyle, D., & Elgie, R. (2016). Maximizing the Reliability of Cross-National Measures of Presidential Power. *British Journal of Political Science, 46*(4), 731–741.

Duverger, M. (1980). A New Political System Model: Semi-Presidential Government. *European Journal of Political Research, 8*(2), 165–187.

Duvold, K., & Jurkynas, M. (2004). Lithuania. In S. Berglund, J. Ekman, & F. H. Aarebrot (Eds.), *The Handbook of Political Change in Eastern Europe* (2nd ed., pp. 133–179). Cheltenham: Edward Elgar.

Ekman, J., Duvold, K., & Berglund, S. (2014). *Baltic Barometer 2014* [Datafile]. Huddinge: Södertörn University.

Ekman, J., Duvold K., & Berglund, S. (2016). *Social-Political Survey in Central Europe* [Datafile]. Huddinge: Södertörn University.

Elgie, R. (Ed.). (1999). *Semi-Presidentialism in Europe*. Oxford: Oxford University Press.

Elgie, R. (2010). Semi-Presidentialism, Cohabitation and the Collapse of Electoral Democracies 1990–2008. *Government and Opposition, 45*(1), 29–49.

Elgie, R. (2011). *Semi-Presidentialism: Sub-Types and Democratic Performance*. Oxford: Oxford University Press.

Elgie, R. (2016). Three Waves of Semi-Presidential Studies. *Democratization, 22*(7), 1–22.

Elgie, R. (2018a). *Political Leadership: A Pragmatic Institutionalist Approach*. London: Palgrave Macmillan.

Elgie, R. (2018b). List of Cohabitations. *The Semi-Presidential One*. Blog Post by Robert Elgie. www.semipresidentialism.com. Accessed 7 Oct 2018.

Elgie, R., & McMenamin, I. (2011). Explaining the Onset of Cohabitation Under Semi-Presidentialism. *Political Studies, 59*(3), 616–635.

Elgie, R., & Moestrup, S. (Eds.). (2008). *Semi-Presidentialism in Central and Eastern Europe*. Manchester: Manchester University Press.

Elgie, R., & Moestrup, S. (Eds.). (2016). *Semi-Presidentialism in the Caucasus and Central Asia*. London: Palgrave Macmillan.

Freedom House. Freedom in the World 2017. www.freedomhouse.org. Accessed 27 Jan 2017.

Gherghina, S., & Miscoiu, S. (2013). The Failure of Cohabitation: Explaining the 2007 and 2012 Institutional Crises in Romania. *East European Politics & Societies and Cultures, 27*(4), 668–684.

Hicken, A., & Stoll, H. (2013). Are All Presidents Created Equal? Presidential Powers and the Shadow of Presidential Elections. *Comparative Political Studies, 46*(3), 291–319.

Lazardeux, S. G. (2015). *Cohabitation and Conflicting Politics in French Policymaking.* Basingstoke: Palgrave Macmillan.

Moestrup, S. (2007). Semi-Presidentialism in Young Democracies: Help or Hindrance? In R. Elgie & S. Moestrup (Eds.), *Semi-Presidentialism Outside Europe* (pp. 30–55). London: Routledge.

New Europe Barometer 2001. (2016). NDB VI Autumn. Dataset SPP 364. CSPP School of Government & Public Policy at the University of Strathclyde. www.cspp.strath.ac.uk/nebo.html. Accessed 15 Sept 2016.

New Europe Barometer 2004. (2016). NDB VII Winter. Dataset SPP 404. CSPP School of Government & Public Policy at the University of Strathclyde. www.cspp.strath.ac.uk/nebo.html. Accessed 15 Sept 2016.

Passarelli, G. (Ed.). (2015). *The Presidentialization of Political Parties: Organizations, Institutions and Leaders.* Basingstoke: Palgrave Macmillan.

Peters, G. (2012). *Institutional Theory in Political Science* (3rd ed.). London: Pinter.

Protsyk, O. (2005). Politics of Intra-Executive Conflict in Semi-Presidential Regimes in Eastern Europe. *East European Politics and Society, 18*(2), 1–20.

Protsyk, O. (2006). Intra-Executive Competition Between President and Prime Minister: Patterns of Institutional Conflict and Cooperation in Semi-Presidential Regimes. *Political Studies, 56*(2), 219–241.

Raunio, T. (2012). Semi-Presidentialism and European Integration: Lessons from Finland for Constitutional Design. *Journal of European Public Policy, 19*(4), 567–584.

Raunio, T., & Sedelius, T. (2017). Shifting Power-Centres of Semi-Presidentialism: Exploring Executive Coordination in Lithuania. *Government and Opposition,* First view. https://doi.org/10.1017/gov.2017.31.

Samuels, D. J., & Shugart, M. S. (2010). *Presidents, Parties, and Prime Ministers: How the Separation of Powers Affects Party Organization and Behavior.* Cambridge: Cambridge University Press.

Schleiter, P., & Morgan-Jones, E. (2009). Citizens, Presidents, and Assemblies: The Study of Semi-Presidentialism Beyond Duverger and Linz. *British Journal of Political Science, 39*(4), 871–892.

Schleiter, P., & Morgan-Jones, E. (2010). Who's in Charge? Presidents, Assemblies, and the Political Control of Semipresidential Cabinets. *Comparative Political Studies, 43*(11), 1415–1441.

Sedelius, T. (2015). Party Presidentialization in Ukraine. In G. Passarelli (Ed.), *The Presidentialization of Political Parties: Organizations, Institutions and Leaders* (pp. 124–141). New York: Palgrave Macmillan.

Sedelius, T. (2016). Ukrainas konstitutionella sicksackande: Regimförändring och partiutveckling under semipresidentialism. *Nordisk Østforum, 30*(1), 18–37.

Sedelius, T., & Åberg, J. (2018). Eastern Europe's Semi-Presidential Regimes. In P. Kopecky & A. Fagan (Eds.), *Routledge Handbook of East European Politics* (pp. 67–81). New York: Routledge.

Sedelius, T., & Ekman, J. (2010). Intra-Executive Conflict and Cabinet Instability: Effects of Semi-Presidentialism in Central and Eastern Europe. *Government and Opposition, 45*(4), 505–530.

Sedelius, T., & Linde, J. (2018). Unravelling Semi-Presidentialism: Democracy and Government Performance in Four Distinct Regime Types. *Democratization, 25*(1), 136–157.

Sedelius, T., & Mashtaler, O. (2013). Two Decades of Semi-Presidentialism: Issues of Intra-Executive Conflict in Central and Eastern Europe 1991–2011. *East European Politics, 29*(2), 109–134.

Shen, Y. (2011). Semi-Presidentialism in Taiwan: A Shadow of the Constitution of the Weimar Republic. *Taiwan Journal of Democracy, 7*(1), 135–152.

Shoesmith, D. (2003). Timor-Leste: Divided Leadership in a Semi-Presidential System. *Asian Survey, 43*(2), 231–252.

Shugart, M. S. (2005). Semi-Presidential Systems: Dual Executive And Mixed Authority Patterns. *French Politics, 3*(3), 323–351.

Shugart, M. S., & Carey, J. M. (1992). *Presidents and Assemblies: Constitutional Design and Electoral Dynamics*. New York: Cambridge University Press.

Siaroff, A. (2003). Comparative Presidencies: The Inadequacy of the Presidential, Semi-Presidential and Parliamentary Distinction. *European Journal of Political Research, 42*(3), 287–312.

Skach, C. (2005). Constitutional Origins of Dictatorship and Democracy. *Constitutional Political Economy, 16*(4), 347–368.

Transparency International. (2019). The Corruption Perception Index 2018. http://www.transparency.org. Accessed 10 Jan 2019.

CHAPTER 2

Institutions, Coordination, and Leadership

Semi-presidentialism as a regime type is arguably more prone to executive conflict than parliamentarism or presidentialism in the sense that disputes arise between the president and the prime minister and the government. In parliamentary systems, coalition cabinets see disputes among the governing parties, but such multiparty coalitions are obviously also found in semi-presidential countries. In presidential regimes, conflicts take place mainly between the president and the legislature. Institutional conflicts can be particularly damaging in terms of coherent leadership and policy-making. This is indeed why political scientists have paid attention to how executives and coalition cabinets work and what types of conflict resolution mechanisms they utilize. That body of research indicates that prime ministers and their cabinets use both ex post instruments—such as the government program and other jointly agreed rules—and ex ante mechanisms—such as various ministerial committees or meetings between leaders of coalition partners (e.g. Müller and Strøm 2000; Strøm et al. 2008). Similarly, in presidential systems like the United States, it is common for the president and his team to have regular contacts with the Congress in order to solve any disagreements.

Nevertheless, as indicated in the introductory chapter, how such coordination and conflict resolution works in semi-presidential remains uncharted territory. Coordination can take many forms, from more codified legal rules to informal conventions and ad hoc practices. The less it is written down into constitutions, laws, or decrees, the more there is space

© The Author(s) 2020   19
T. Raunio, T. Sedelius, *Semi-Presidential Policy-Making in Europe*,
Palgrave Studies in Presidential Politics,
https://doi.org/10.1007/978-3-030-16431-7_2

for short-term solutions and agenda setting by individual office-holders. Conflict resolution can take place bilaterally between the president and the prime minister, but also between their respective offices and political advisers. The level of coordination can also vary between different policy sectors, with foreign and security policies as particularly challenging areas where both the president and the prime minister usually share powers, and as countries are expected to speak with one voice in external relations.

Embedded in institutional theory and building on four strands of literature (public administration, political leadership, foreign policy analysis, and of course previous studies of semi-presidentialism), this chapter provides the main analytical framework of our book. It starts by outlining key concepts and findings from institutional theory before moving more specifically to the incentives that presidents and prime ministers have for engaging in intra-executive cooperation. The specific challenges related to leadership in foreign and security policy, including EU affairs, are highlighted, especially because in all of the countries examined in this book the directly elected presidents either lead foreign policy or have at least quite considerable powers in that field. In the final section of this chapter, we map out various potential coordination mechanisms and discuss their role in intra-executive relations.

2.1   Institutional Theory and Policy Coordination

Coordination or collective action problems are a key concern of institutional theory studying how institutional design structures social behavior and influences political outcomes. In line with North (1990: 3), "institutions are the rules of the game in a society, or, more formally, are the humanly devised constraints that shape human interaction". Institutions are normally established to reduce the obstacles stemming from incomplete and asymmetrical information, with such obstacles referred to as transaction costs. The concept of path dependency is commonly utilized to explain why certain institutional models are adopted, and it emphasizes that initially adopted policies or organizational solutions become the appropriate course of action and, as "rules of the game", structure political behavior with the consequence that "particular courses of action, once introduced, can be virtually impossible to reverse" (Pierson 2000: 251). Feedback in turn is closely linked to path dependency, for it means that "once a set of institutions is in place, actors adapt their strategies in ways that reflect but also reinforce the 'logic' of the system" (Thelen 1999:

392). As a result, institutional arrangements tend to reproduce the distribution of power in political systems (e.g. North 1990; Goodin 1996; Hall and Taylor 1996; Pierson 2000; Rhodes et al. 2006; Lowndes and Roberts 2013; Scott 2014).

Institutions are thus known for their longevity, with institutional changes normally brought about by critical junctures. As the word 'critical' implies, this concept stresses that the event leading to institutional change must be sufficiently significant to overcome the path dependency and stickiness of institutions. According to an often-used definition, a critical juncture is "a period of significant change … which is hypothesized to produce distinct legacies" (Collier and Collier 1991: 29). Obviously, the institutionalist literature can be criticized for being vague or unclear on what constitutes a critical juncture, but examples could be constitutional reform processes, policy failures or gridlocks, or severe economic recessions (Thelen 1999).

Effective institutions reduce transaction costs and uncertainty in exchange, so that individuals are aware of and can anticipate each other's preferences and behavior. Institutions can thus make a difference in that they induce actors otherwise driven by self-interest toward a problem-solving mode characterized by cooperation and search for mutually beneficial solutions (Scharpf 1989). In line with the rational choice variant of institutionalism, we "postulate, first, that an actor's behavior is likely to be driven, not by impersonal historical forces, but by a strategic calculus and, second, that this calculus will be deeply affected by the actor's expectations about how others are likely to behave as well. Institutions structure such interactions, by affecting the range and sequence of alternatives on the choice-agenda or by providing information and enforcement mechanisms that reduce uncertainty about the corresponding behavior of others and allow 'gains from exchange', thereby leading actors toward particular calculations and potentially better social outcomes" (Hall and Taylor 1996: 945). Institutions should also facilitate long-term considerations. Politicians are arguably particularly motivated by re-election, and this contributes to office-holders prioritizing short-term gains. Institutions can thus lengthen the time horizons of politicians through creating conditions for credible commitments, particularly when the game is repeated and interaction is regular among a small number of participants (North 1990, 1993).

Long-term, stable repeated interaction should also strengthen the sociological or cultural explanations of institutions. The logic of appropriateness, initially developed by March and Olsen (1989, 2004,

2006), perceives political activity as the product of matching behavioral norms to situations and highlights the rule-driven and socially embedded nature of human (inter)actions: "To act appropriately is to proceed according to the institutionalized practices of a collectivity, based on mutual, and often tacit, understandings of what is true, reasonable, natural, right, and good" (March and Olsen 2004: 4). In a nutshell, an individual approaches a situation by interpreting it in the light of one's professional identity and context, evaluates the appropriateness of different courses of action, and then selects the alternative that is perceived as the most appropriate. Hence, the logic of appropriateness is also connected to the socialization effects of institutions, with individuals becoming accustomed to the organizational norms and "ways of doing things". Key elements of the logic of appropriateness are thus rules, social identity, and the recognition of situations (Messick 1999). In contrast with the identity-based logic of appropriateness, the logic of consequences action is more preference-driven and guided by outcomes. That is, an individual or group chooses the alternative with the highest expected pay-off. Distinguishing between two such behavioral logics can be difficult (Goldmann 2005), but again the main point is that rules are likely to be sustained as long as they are perceived both legitimate and efficient by the relevant actors.

Formal and Informal Institutions

As explained above, institutions are essentially "the rules of the game" that guide and constrain human interaction. However, these rules of the game can be either *formal* or *informal* institutions. Following North and others, there is broad consensus that formal rules are written down and created by state institutions, typically legislatures, executives, or courts, and also enforced through official channels. Hence, they are easily traceable. Defining and identifying informal institutions is considerably trickier (Lauth 2015). Again following North and subsequent research, we define informal institutions as "socially shared rules, usually unwritten, that are created, communicated, and enforced outside of officially sanctioned channels" (Helmke and Levitsky 2004: 727). To be sure, separating formal and informal institutions is often very difficult, but for our purposes this approach, based on the distinction between official and unofficial rules, is sufficient as we are interested in the interaction between formal rules and real-world practice.

Informal institutions can obviously have both positive and negative effects on democracy and decision-making. They can prove functional and have beneficial effects on decision-making and the stability or performance of formal institutions, or informal institutions can be dysfunctional in that they actually undermine problem-solving or destabilize cooperation and formal institutions. Good examples of the former are various informal routines or conventions adopted by individual political institutions such as legislative committees or bureaucracies, or indeed the ways in which the coordination between the president and the Congress has evolved over the decades (Riggs 1988). Examples of dysfunctional informal institutions also abound, not least such deep-seated practices as clientelism or corruption that undermine economy and political legitimacy.

Expanding on the work of Lauth (2000), Helmke and Levitsky (2004, 2006b) have produced a more fine-grained categorization of informal institutions, distinguishing between *complementary, accommodating, competing*, and *substitutive* institutions. Their typology also has two dimensions: whether formal and informal institutions produce convergent or divergent outcomes, and whether or not formal rules are effective, that is, complied with and enforced. *Complementary institutions* combine effective formal institutions and convergent outcomes. "Such institutions 'fill in gaps' either by addressing contingencies not dealt with in the formal rules or by facilitating the pursuit of individual goals within the formal institutional framework. These informal institutions often enhance efficiency" (Helmke and Levitsky 2004: 728). Importantly, "by enhancing the performance of formal institutions or increasing the benefits gained by working within them, complementary informal institutions may strengthen actors' commitment to formal rules" (Helmke and Levitsky 2006b: 17). *Accommodating institutions* in turn combine effective formal institutions and divergent outcomes: they "create incentives to behave in ways that alter the substantive effects of formal rules, but without directly violating them; they contradict the spirit, but not the letter, of the formal rules. Accommodating informal institutions are often created by actors who dislike outcomes generated by the formal rules but are unable to change or openly violate those rules. As such, they often help to reconcile these actors' interests with the existing formal institutional arrangements" (Helmke and Levitsky 2004: 729). For example, Siavelis (2006) has shown how in Chile the political elites, unable to amend the constitution, created various informal power-sharing institutions that counteracted the constitutionally extremely strong presidency and thereby contributed to the stability of the political regime. As a result of such informal rules, Chilean presidents in fact, unlike most of the Latin American presidents, systematically refrained from making most of their constitutional prerogatives. *Competing institutions* are the third category: such institutions, like corruption mentioned above, are incompatible with formal rules. Fourth, *substitutive informal institutions* combine ineffective formal institutions and convergent outcomes. Existing mainly in contexts where formal institutions are not enforced, they are established to achieve what formal institutions do not deliver.

As already outlined in Chap. 1, one of the main lessons to be drawn from existing literature on semi-presidentialism is that the real-world influence of presidents can hardly be deduced from the wording of the constitution. One of our central arguments is that it is not sufficient to study formal rules—one must go beyond them to the level of informal institutions and practices in order to understand how semi-presidential regimes operate. As Helmke and Levitsky (2004: 734) argue more broadly about comparative politics: "In comparative politics, the issue of how informal institutions sustain or reinforce—as opposed to undermine or distort—formal ones has not been well researched. When institutions function effectively, we often assume that the formal rules are driving actors' behavior. Yet in some cases, underlying informal norms do much of the enabling and constraining that we attribute to the formal rules." Informal institutions can often be even more important than the formal ones, especially in developing countries and other less stable contexts. Referring to the Latin American experiences, Helmke and Levitsky (2006a: 281) even argue that "the failure of presidentialism in many developing countries may be rooted not only in the existence of subversive informal institutions such as patrimonialism ... but also in the absence of the complementary informal institutions needed to sustain it". Hence, we expect to find stronger evidence of such informal rules in the younger Central European democracies than in Finland. In line with institutionalist literature, we examine informal institutions at two different levels—the broader society or political system and the actual intra-executive coordination. The former level should be understood as contextual features that influence how political regimes operate, such as personalization of politics or excessive clientelism and corruption. When examining intra-executive cooperation, our focus in turn is on the various informal mechanisms that facilitate or do not facilitate effective power-sharing decision-making.

This leads us to the emergence and identification of informal institutions. We again follow Helmke and Levitsky (2004: 730), according to whom "actors create informal rules because formal institutions are incomplete. Formal rules set general parameters for behavior, but they cannot cover all contingencies. Consequently, actors operating within a particular formal institutional context, such as bureaucracies and legislatures, develop norms and procedures that expedite their work or address problems not anticipated by formal rules." Elite-level informal rules involving only a small number of actors are also likelier to change or to be abolished than broader, societal informal institutions (Helmke and Levitsky 2006b: 22). Hence, there needs to be shared expectations or understandings among the relevant actors about the costs and benefits of the informal institution. Regarding identification at the level of intra-executive relations, a prerequisite in our context is that the relevant actors—primarily the two executives and probably also the broader political elite—recognize the institution as something more than a merely ad hoc arrangement dependent on individual office-holders. This is indeed one of the reasons why our primary material is interviews with top-level politicians and civil servants in the three countries.

To conclude, both formal and informal institutions are purposeful creations of human beings. They are obviously established under conditions of incomplete information and, particularly through critical junctures may either be abolished altogether or be significantly reformed. But if, on the other hand, they prove successful, even those actors that were initially against the design of the institution may come to regard it as a legitimate rule guiding their actions. Hence, institutions should always serve the interests of their creators and/or the key actors involved (Greif and Kingston 2011). In semi-presidential regimes, this primarily means the presidents and prime ministers.

2.2   Semi-Presidentialism and the Challenge of Cooperation

But why would the president and the prime minister adhere to common institutions—or why would they seek cooperation and institutional constraints to begin with? We approach this question first from the perspective of alternative party goals developed by Strøm (1990; see Müller and Strøm 1999). That framework distinguishes between office-seeking, policy-seeking, and vote-seeking models of party behavior. Office-seeking parties seek to maximize their control over benefits that can be derived from holding public office. Office-seeking behavior thus aims at winning public office, mainly operationalized as participation in the government. Policy-seeking parties, on the other hand, seek to maximize their impact on public policy. The success of a party in achieving that can be measured by the extent to which it can change public policy toward its own preferred position (or to prevent undesirable outcomes). Most of the literature has seen policy-seeking behavior to be secondary to office-seeking behavior, as influencing public policy is probably best achieved through being in the government (e.g. Lazardeux 2015). Vote-seeking parties in turn seek to maximize their share of the votes in elections.

The Incentives for Coordination

While the framework of alternative goals was developed with political parties in mind, the same logic can be applied to semi-presidential regimes. Regarding policy influence, cooperation can benefit both the president and the prime minister as institutional theory informs us. Regular coordination of the two executives enables them to learn each other's preferences and bargaining styles. It facilitates the identification and solving of problematic questions, with both sides able to address potential grievances ex ante before the more formal or public decision-making stage. If the prime minister wants to avoid interference from the president, she better coordinate with the president before matters are introduced. Moreover, if the president wants to shape policy, especially over a longer term, then coordination is probably a better strategy than public confrontation. Through coordination, policy gridlocks are avoided and successful policy-making, for example in terms of economic growth or smooth foreign relations, should benefit both sides. Moreover, willingness to cooperate is often regarded as a sign of statesmanship and maturity, especially in foreign and security policy (see the next section), qualities that should enhance the re-election prospects of both the president and the prime minister.

Incumbents are at the same time constrained by existing rules and by external factors. Incoming presidents or prime ministers of course inherit modes of operation from their predecessors. In line with path dependency, coordination may be a well-established practice and regulated by the constitution or other laws, in which case unilateral rejection of cooperation by new office-holders is difficult. Time constraints are also likely to favor coordination based on clear rules, as policy processes are often character-ized by tight and unpredictable deadlines. While domestic political calen-dars can be altered, for example, in terms of when to introduce new legislative bills, similar rights do not normally extend to European or global negotiations and developments. If the president and the prime min-ister are both involved in EU or foreign affairs, then regular coordination makes it possible to react quickly to changing external circumstances.

The Ultimate Goal of Winning Office

Coordination and overall smooth intra-executive relations thus have clear benefits, especially in terms of policy-making. Yet when it comes to vote-seeking, the question we ask is what kind of behavior facilitates the winning of public office. There are sometimes good reasons for presidents and prime ministers motivated by re-election or winning office not to enter into coop-eration or, despite coordination mechanisms, to "go public" with their opin-ion differences, especially when they need to either claim credit or avoid blame for particular policies. In his analysis of American presidents, Kernell (2007: 1–2) defines going public as "a strategy whereby a president pro-motes himself and his policies in Washington by appealing directly to the American public for support". Importantly, Kernell (2007: 3–4) also empha-sizes that going public is directly at odds with bargaining with the Congress and other political actors and institutions. Through public speeches and writings, the president "seeks the aid of a third party—the public—to force other politicians to accept his preferences". It also entails public posturing, and "to the extent that it fixes the president's bargaining position, posturing makes subsequent compromise with other politicians more difficult". Furthermore, "and possibly most injurious to bargaining, going public undermines the legitimacy of other politicians". Presidents are typically more popular than prime ministers and other party politicians, and hence aggres-sive use of powers invested in the presidency and public grandstanding may work in their favor, particularly if the government is suffering from low pop-ularity ratings. As for prime ministers, direct criticism of the head of state is under normal conditions not perceived as appropriate. But should the presi-dent in turn be unpopular, for example, through corruption scandals, then a more confrontational strategy vis-à-vis the president might be feasible.

The weight of such strategic calculations should not be underestimated. After all, both presidents and prime ministers are typically ambitious and experienced politicians who know both the intricacies and the bigger picture of how politics operates in their countries. They not only understand the constitutional framework, but also how party-political factors and the broader political culture influence the distribution of power. For example, Lazardeux (2015) shows how electoral motives, particularly winning presidential elections, the main prize in French politics, have shaped the strategies of both executives. The president and the prime minister thus know the "rules of the game" and, whether driven by winning or staying in office, policy influence, or re-election, shapes their behavior accordingly.

President's Toolbox and Contextual Determinants

Obviously, variation on formal presidential powers goes a long way in explaining key differences between semi-presidential regimes as well as in determining the power balance between the president and the prime minister. Hence, we will detail quite carefully the constitutional powers of the president in the subsequent empirical chapters. As there are also many different alternatives in the literature on how to measure presidential powers, we will present some of these in Chap. 3. At this point, however, we may use Chaisty et al. (2018) just to illustrate broad clusters of presidential powers that the president may or may not have, or may have but only under certain restrictions. Chaisty et al. separate between agenda power (legislative powers, e.g. initiative of legislative bills, decree, and veto), budgetary prerogatives (control of public spending), cabinet management (formation and dismissal powers, distribution of minister portfolios), partisan powers (influence of the president over parties), and informal institutions (a diverse residual category, reflecting country-specific historical and cultural factors). While Chaisty et al. study presidential regimes in Latin America and president-parliamentary regimes in post-Soviet countries, where all these power clusters are more or less relevant, we are interested in premier-presidential regimes in Europe with considerably weaker presidencies. Hence, to our cases, agenda power in certain defined policy areas, cabinet management in terms of government formation, the president's partisan power, and again informal institutions are of particular relevance.

But whether presidents use, or indeed need to use, their formal prerogatives depends on various contextual factors. Party-political disagreements are the fundamental obstacle to successful coordination. As outlined in Chap. 1, cohabitation is defined as a situation where the prime minister and the president represent opposing parties and where the party of the president is not included in the government (Elgie 2018). Under cohabitation, the president and the prime minister are ideologically often quite far apart, and even when there is intra-executive coordination, presidents can in the end choose to exercise their right of veto over legislation or appointments or publicly criticize the government's policies while prime ministers may try to push through legislation they know will not please the president. The president and the prime minister thus need to signal to their voters that while intra-executive compromises have been adopted, not everything is for sale and that they care about issues that are salient among their electorates. Under unified government, in turn, the president and the prime minister represent the same party or at least are not from opposing ideological blocs. As Samuels and Shugart (2010) and Passarelli (2015) have shown, under such situations the president in premier-presidential regimes can wield strong influence over the government, both through her power of selecting and/or deselecting the prime minister or simply through intra-party decision-making processes. Hence, the authors talk about the "presidentialization" of political parties.

Nor can one disregard other contextual variables. Presidential activism tends to be higher when the country is experiencing political turbulence, with low level of societal consensus or weak governments (e.g. Tavits 2009). As argued in Chap. 3, these considerations are particularly relevant for the newer democracies in Central and Eastern Europe, where surveys show high levels of public trust in the presidents but outright distrust in other political leaders such as the prime minister and the parties. The presidents' greater popularity may be attributed to their limited powers and to their status as being above party politics, elevated from the usual political quarrels. Prime ministers, on the contrary, experience the dilemma of exercising their power in areas of controversy, such as social and economic policies, thereby often eroding their popular support. The paradox, however, is that the presidents may experience that their popularity outweigh their formal powers and their de facto political influence. When seeking ways of converting their perceived prestige into actual power, they have the option of going public to criticize the government. Hence, formally weak presidents may thus compensate their limited constitutional powers with more indirect channels of influence or even obtrusive behavior.

Hence, the president and the prime minister should have stronger incentives to seek cooperation when there is a more balanced distribution of power between the two executives and/or if the two executives share powers in a particular policy area. When the government is clearly dominant, then the prime minister can feel no need for coordination beyond perhaps the president's office receiving information about governmental decisions and policies. Under power-sharing in turn there are simply more issues subject to joint decision-making, thereby providing an incentive for intra-executive coordination. To be sure, there are thus also more possibilities for disagreement, but regular cooperation should facilitate successful policy-making. The latter applies especially to foreign and security policies, including EU affairs, issue areas where it is often emphasized that disunity at home should not undermine success abroad.

Finally, one should not forget the impact of personalities or leadership styles. One way to examine presidential activism is to distinguish between presidency-centered and president-centered explanations. The former refers to studies that approach presidential behavior through constitutional powers and the political context, while the latter emphasizes the role of individual office-holders and their personalities (Hager and Sullivan 1994; Gilmour 2002; Köker 2017: 23–54). President-centered explanations are thus linked to agency, another central concept in institutional theory (e.g. Lowndes and Roberts 2013: 77–110). Political actors can interpret rules differently or try to bend them in their favor without directly violating the formal or informal institutions, such as constitutional division of powers. Some presidents may choose to sit back and let the prime minister rule, whereas others will seek to maximize their political influence. This underlines the need to compare not just between semi-presidential regimes but also over-time developments in individual countries. This is obviously another key lesson to be drawn from previous research on semi-presidentialism, particularly in the context of less stable regimes such as many countries in East and Central Europe.

2.3   Foreign Policy and the Challenge of Leadership

Examining semi-presidentialism and intra-executive coordination is ultimately research about leadership. If, as the literature indicates (see Chap. 1), semi-presidentialism is more prone to executive conflict than parliamentary or presidential systems, then semi-presidentialism as a regime type poses certain leadership problems. Students of political leadership normally emphasize that the leader of a political entity such as a country or a particular organization should provide clear and sufficiently dynamic leadership, especially during times that are more difficult. Communication plays an important role in modern leadership, with leaders expected to justify their positions and inform the electorate through a variety of channels (Helms 2012; Rhodes and 't Hart 2014).

Speaking with One Voice

The external relations of a country, encompassing foreign and security policy as well as EU matters, pose particular challenges for leadership because of three interrelated factors. First, as mentioned in the previous section, individual countries cannot dictate the timetable of regional (EU) or international bargaining or events. International politics are full of unexpected crises, from terrorist attacks to major natural disasters, to which countries are expected to react, either alone or as part of an alliance such as EU or NATO. For example, in recent years developments in Syria or Russia have necessitated quick responses from the international community. More importantly, membership in the European Union or international organizations comes with its own set of constraints. In the EU, the member states need to formulate national negotiating stances ahead of Council and European Council meetings. The role of the European Council and other summits between political leaders of member states has accentuated in recent years through issues such as the euro crisis, the refugee movement from the Middle East and Africa, and Brexit, with many of these summits convened at a short notice. NATO countries face similar pressures, while in global organizations like the World Trade Organization (WTO), bargaining is less regular, but nonetheless countries again need to decide on their positions in advance of negotiation rounds.

Second, in external relations countries are expected to speak with one voice. Even when there is vibrant domestic debate, countries should formulate a single negotiating position that is subsequently defended abroad. Hence, there is a special need for coherence in foreign affairs. This is also why it is customary to argue that foreign policy is or should be very much the special domain of the executive, as the involvement of domestic actors such as legislatures might produce unnecessary delays or create confusion about the national position. This line of thinking is nothing new and can be traced back to political philosophers such as Locke (1960) or de Tocqueville (1990). The 'special case' of foreign affairs can be best captured through comparing it with domestic policies. In domestic issues party-political conflicts and public discussion are seen as normal and necessary for democratic deliberation, whereas foreign policy decision-makers often evoke notions of national unity demanding that major political parties at least try to build consensus in order not to jeopardize the success of the executive that represents the country in bilateral talks or in international bargaining. This is indeed the core of the 'politics stops at the water's edge' idiom, according to which ideological differences are set aside in favor of national interest (Raunio and Wagner 2017).

Security and the National Interest

This brings us to the third factor, which is the sensitive nature of security and defense policies. It is only logical that questions related to national security would be particularly important for any country. And for many if not most countries, there is in foreign and security policy a core 'national interest' that forms the *raison d'être* of the country in international relations. This core national interest might result from geographical location (such as proximity to an unfriendly neighbor), past historical events (such as experience of the Second World War), or military alliances (such as NATO). In such cases, there is often broad partisan and societal consensus behind the national interest. Domestic actors like political parties or individual office-holders may nonetheless differ in their interpretations of that national interest and how much it binds them. Furthermore, changes in the neighboring region or in the international system may result in even quite fundamental rethinking of the interests of the country (e.g. Rosenau 1971; Finnemore 1996; Hill 2013).

For all of the countries covered in this volume, relations with Russia and the 'Cold War era' experiences have been of utmost salience, explaining or at least strongly influencing decisions about whether to join military alliances. Issues concerning national armies, including whether countries should take part in international crisis management operations, are likewise salient as the executive needs to make careful judgments about troop deployments and their potential consequences. In these kinds of security and military matters, secrecy and confidentiality are often presented as integral to the advancement of national interests. Domestic consensus is valued, and the public seems to appreciate "solid" leadership, with the executive given room for maneuver to ensure that national security is not compromised. International crises thus bring about, at least temporarily, a rally-around-the-flag effect (Mueller 1973; O'Neal et al. 1996).

Furthermore, executives can seek to avoid domestic constraints through framing issues as security threats—in line with what is termed 'securitization' in international relations literature (Waever 1995; Buzan et al. 1998).

In the United States, presidents have benefited from framing foreign policy issues as security or military matters or from employing the rhetoric of war in other issue areas such as fighting drugs. During wars presidents enjoy not only more discretion but also greater success in navigating policies through the Congress, and budgetary items with more direct connections to national security allow the president greater freedom from Congressional constraints than foreign trade and aid (e.g. Howell et al. 2013; Milner and Tingley 2015). In the semi-presidential regimes covered in this book, economic or energy relations with Russia could be an example of an issue where the leader of foreign policy seeks to expand her influence through presenting ties with Russia as an issue of national security.

These considerations suggest that there is a stronger need for intra-executive coordination in foreign and security policy. Indeed, individual countries often use special coordination instruments in these policy areas. Apart from ministerial committees, there can be defense councils or their equivalents, bringing together representatives from the political leadership, the bureaucracy, and the armed forces to periodically review security developments. Another institutional mechanism worthy of attention is the 'grand strategy' document, which is often decided in or at least shaped by discussions in a specific ministerial committee or the defense council. Countries throughout the world, as well as NATO and the EU, have adopted grand strategies that outline the core objectives and issues in foreign and security policy. Good examples are the Nordic countries, where essentially all political parties represented in the legislatures are actively involved in the formulation of the grand strategy documents (Drent and Meijnders 2015; Raunio 2016). The question of who chairs such bodies or leads these processes is thus significant in terms of the balance of power between the president and the prime minister.

EU and the Potential for Jurisdictional Disputes

EU matters fall somewhere in-between domestic and foreign affairs: while the deepening of integration, together with recent crises (notably those affecting the euro area), has brought about quite significant politicization and contestation about European issues, the domestic policy-making culture in EU affairs is nonetheless more executive-driven and confidential than in domestic policies (Hegeland 2007). Member states have established domestic EU coordination systems that particularly emphasize the formulation of national positions ahead of European-level meetings, but such studies have for the most part not paid attention to the role of the president (Kassim et al. 2000; Bulmer and Lequesne 2013; but see Leuffen 2009).

However, not only is the EU highly important for the countries examined in this book, we also argue that the domestic management of EU issues can in fact prove particularly problematic for semi-presidential member states. The biggest challenge is posed by jurisdictional disputes and the competition for authority. In several semi-presidential countries, both the government and the president are involved in national foreign and/or European policy. In most of these countries, the government is in charge of European policy, with the competence of the president limited to foreign and defense policies. Yet the main difficulty lies in drawing a clear line between EU and foreign policies. National foreign policies are increasingly influenced by and linked to EU, and hence the foreign policy powers of the presidents are circumscribed by the ongoing development of the EU's Common Foreign and Security Policy and Common Security and Defence Policy (CFSP/CSDP). As a result, presidents arguably have a legitimate justification for becoming more strongly involved in European affairs, for example through the question of who represents the country in the European Council or in other European-level summits, or how the president should be involved in the national EU coordination system. This in turn produces jurisdictional conflicts, as the government (supported by its majority in the parliament) will defend its turf against presidential encroachments. And even if the role of the president is more ceremonial in foreign or EU affairs, the presidents can be veto players in Treaty amendments, or through being the Commander-in-Chief of the Armed Forces, they can wield influence in crisis management operations and in the overall development of EU's military dimension. It hence appears that in semi-presidential systems domestic strains will be the inevitable outcome when the formal rules vest the direction of foreign and/or EU policy conjointly in the president and the government (Raunio 2012).

2.4   Theoretical Framework and Coordination Mechanisms

Figure 2.1 summarizes our basic theoretical argument. We understand coordination instruments as intervening variables positioned between key explanatory factors derived from previous literature (constitutional powers, party politics, and societal context) and the level of presidential activ-

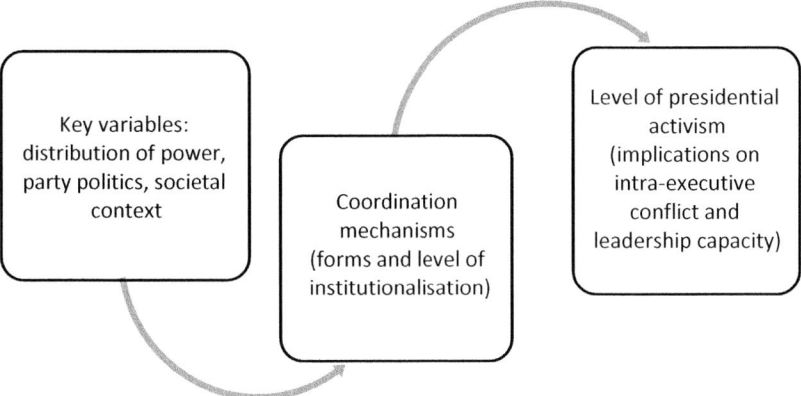

Fig. 2.1 Theoretical framework: executive coordination and presidential activism

ism and distribution of power inside the executive. But before proceeding any further, we must define what we mean by 'presidential activism'. As Köker (2017: 4–5) points out, this concept has mainly been used in scholarship on American presidents, and despite its wide usage no universally accepted definition seems to exist. Köker (2017: 5) himself defines it as "the discretionary use of formal powers by the president". This definition certainly makes sense given that Köker examines presidents' use of veto powers and their role in government formation and censure, prerogatives that are found in the constitutions. However, we are interested not only in how presidents use their constitutionally assigned powers, but also—or perhaps even primarily—in how they try to influence politics through other channels, such as direct appeals to the public or direct contacts to individual ministers and party leaders, the parliament, and its party groups. As a result, our definition is intentionally broader: we define presidential activism as *the presidents' use of their formal powers and their attempts to influence politics through informal channels*. The level of presidential activism in turn is expected to affect the level of intra-executive conflict and overall leadership capacity. The more regular and institutionalized the coordination mechanisms are, the stronger their effect should be.

In line with institutional theory, our working hypothesis is that "institutions matter" (Weaver and Rockman 1993). While we acknowledge the importance of the key variables such as distribution of powers and party politics identified in Fig. 2.1, we argue that institutional mechanisms of executive coordination make a genuine difference: individual office-holders are constrained by them, especially when the mechanisms have become more entrenched and are recognized as legitimate by the actors involved. The literature on political systems or individual decision-making bodies such as legislatures is full of examples of the positive effects of such institutions. Turning more specifically to semi-presidentialism, the most famous representative of the regime type, France, illustrates how coordination mechanisms can at least moderate conflicts between the president and the prime minister. According to Elgie (2001), intra-executive relations in the French Fifth Republic have been characterized by both conflict and compromise, with the former manifesting itself in different ways, including in a degree of political gridlock, in an increased use of extraordinary constitutional, administrative, and political procedures, and in an ongoing battle for public opinion. During unified government, presidential advisers have routinely attended government meetings, whereas under cohabitation they have not (with the exception of certain defense and foreign policy meetings). Instead, the president and the prime minister have met on a weekly basis, prior to the government meetings. The existence of regular channels for communication secures that even during public confrontations common tasks can still be carried out and inconvenient mistakes may be avoided.

In contrast, when coordination instruments do not exist or are weak, then both executives have more freedom of maneuver. Absent of a working constitutional division of labor and coordination, particularly the presidents are more likely to use alternative channels of influence—such as the strategy of going public or direct contacts with political parties, the legislature, or civil society stakeholders—and to intervene in questions falling under the competence of the government. Furthermore, ad hoc practices are likely to favor the side that, either because of constitutional division of power or through contextual factors, enjoys agenda-setting powers and can thus choose or at least strongly influence the levels and forms of coordination.

We hypothesize that institutional design is related to the level of presidential activism and that intra-executive conflicts over policy, legislation, or appointments are often manifestations of coordination problems. These intra-executive conflicts can be clearly observable and manifest such as through public disputes between the president and the prime minister, legislative vetoes by the president, and clashes over cabinet appointments or performance. However, drawing on our top-level expert interviews in the three countries, we can also uncover conflicts that occur "behind the scenes", causing tensions on both sides that can but do not necessarily result in more public confrontations.

Institutions of Executive Coordination: An Explorative Model

The last part of this chapter outlines various coordinative institutions that can be used for intra-executive coordination in semi-presidential regimes. We do not claim this list to be exhaustive—rather it is an early and tentative framework to be tested on our subsequent empirical analysis in Chaps. 4, 5 and 6. We identify three levels of coordination—*bilateral* (between the president and the prime minister), *collective* (between the president and the government), and *administrative* (between the office of the president and the office of the prime minister and the ministries)—while also differentiating among policy areas. We introduce the coordination instruments one by one, identifying also their predicted roles in intra-executive coordination (Fig. 2.2).

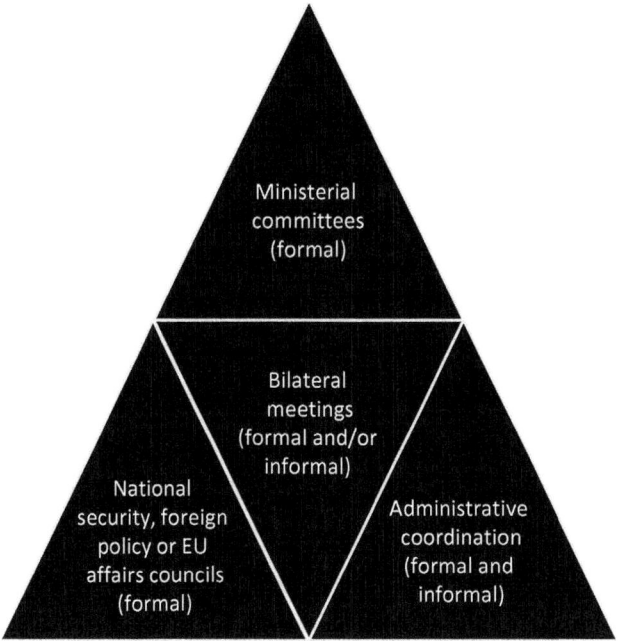

Fig. 2.2   Institutions of executive coordination: a tentative model

Bilateral Meetings Between the President and Prime Minister We assign particular importance to confidential exchanges between the two leaders that form the core of intra-executive coordination. Hence, this type of coordination is in the center of Fig. 2.2, whereas the other mechanisms should on average be less crucial, particularly in terms of solving intra-executive conflicts. Regular talks between the president and the prime minister enable them to learn about each other's preferences, negotiation styles, and personalities. Such face-to-face contacts should ideally take place before the president meets the whole government or before either side meets foreign leaders or attends international or EU meetings. In this way, potentially sensitive issues can be discussed in private, and even if no compromise is found, both leaders can agree on how to proceed with these matters. However, it is unlikely that laws would regulate such bilateral meetings, and hence they should primarily be seen as informal institutions, particularly if their existence is not dependent on individual office-holders. More specifically, bilateral meetings should be regarded as complementary informal institutions, as they are designed to improve coordination between the two executives. However, the informal nature of bilateral exchanges makes them also vulnerable to breaking down after the election of new office-holders.

Ministerial Committees or Joint Councils Between the President and the Government As the literature on coalition governments shows, ministerial committees perform an important function in both cabinet decision-making and as a conflict resolution mechanism (Müller and Strøm 2000; Strøm et al. 2008). These ministerial committees typically bring together a subset of ministers from all coalition parties and they deal with specific issue areas such as economic policy or European policy. The powers and composition of the ministerial committees are often regulated by laws or even by constitutions, with more detailed rules found in the government's rules of procedure, and hence they are formal institutions. In policy areas where the president shares power with the government, mainly in foreign and security policy, such ministerial committees would enable both sides to keep track of developments and to exchange ideas before the formal decision-making stage. Various joint councils would on average have a more informal status. These councils would again bring together the president and ministers to discuss specific societal issues such as education or economy. They could also take the form of periodic meetings between the whole government and the president that would focus perhaps mainly on topical issues.

National Security, Foreign Policy, or EU Affairs Councils External relations were identified as a policy area where directly elected presidents not only have constitutional powers but where countries are expected to act with one voice. This applies particularly to security and defense policies, issue areas that are highly salient and where domestic consensus is appreciated. National security councils or equivalents could thus be in a central role in defining and planning the countries' security and military strategies. They can simultaneously facilitate intra-executive coordination, but who chairs such bodies can be a delicate question. Naturally, ministerial committees can also be established to examine foreign and security policy and indeed European matters. EU affairs pose particular challenges for coordination, especially as the development of CFSP/CSDP means that national foreign and security policies—areas where presidents enjoy constitutional powers—are increasingly linked to European-level policy processes. Hence, whether the president is involved in or excluded from the national EU coordination system can have broader implications for leadership in foreign affairs. Here we can again find both formal and informal institutions. National security councils should have formal status, whereas the involvement of the president in national EU coordination need not be regulated by any written procedures.

Coordination Between Civil Servants of the Offices of the Prime Minister and the President Moving away from the explicitly 'political' coordination to the administrative level, we also examine interaction between the respective offices of the president and the prime minister. Comparative literature suggests that the role of top-level administrative elites has become more important over the decades. Political leaders have typically two categories of staff working for them: civil servants that work for the state and political staff that come and go with individual office-holders. The staff at the prime minister's office oversees and coordinates activities in the ministries and perhaps also public sector agencies while handling central governmental communication. Particularly the political staff provides policy advice to the prime minister or the president, including in foreign and security policy, and can be a key player in solving disputes between different branches of government (e.g. Mitchell 2005; Eichbaum and Shaw 2014; Yong and Hazell 2014; Gherghina and Kopecký 2016; Marland et al. 2017).

Regular coordination and exchange of information between the staffs of the prime minister and the president should facilitate successful cooperation between the two executives. However, the size and responsibilities of especially the president's staff can also be highly important variables. The budget of the president's office is normally determined by the annual national budget, and in premier-presidential countries, the total number of staff working for the president tends to be quite small. Presidents can compensate this with recruiting personnel to focus on specific policy areas, including those falling in the competence of the government. For example, a policy adviser in economy can provide crucial information to the president and can form contacts with the relevant ministry and parliamentary committee. Furthermore, a small but effective communication staff can be of substantial help in spreading the word about the president's views and activities.

To sum up, the weaker the presence of these coordination mechanisms, the more there is space and need for presidential activism: going public, direct contacts with individual ministers and party leaders, the parliament, and party groups, with the president building these contacts to stay in the loop of governmental activities and to influence decision-making in the cabinet or the legislature. Such contacts can also undermine trust between the prime minister and the president, as the former may feel that the president is bypassing her. Presidents are in most cases elected as candidates of a particular political party or coalition of parties, and hence ties to those parties should naturally be stronger than to the competing parties, also because of the "presidentialization of parties" effect discussed above. Weaker coordination should also increase the likelihood of the president criticizing the cabinet publicly. In terms of institutional theory, such 'going public' strategies should first and foremost be seen as either accommodating or as competing informal institutions. Presidential activism is an accommodating institution if it seeks to expand presidential influence while respecting at least the letter of the constitution. Activism can also be a competing institution if presidential behavior clearly contradicts formal, constitutional division of authority, for example by extensive interference in the formation or work of governments or in parliamentary decision-making.

Bibliography

Bulmer, S., & Lequesne, C. (Eds.). (2013). *The Member States of the European Union* (2nd ed.). Oxford: Oxford University Press.

Buzan, B., Waever, O., & de Wilde, J. (1998). *Security: A Framework for Analysis.* Boulder: Lynne Rienner.

Chaisty, P., Cheeseman, N., & Power, T. J. (2018). *Coalitional Presidentialism in Comparative Perspective: Minority Presidents in Multiparty Systems.* Oxford: Oxford University Press.

Collier, R. B., & Collier, D. (1991). *Shaping the Political Arena: Critical Junctures, the Labor Movement, and Regime Dynamics in Latin America.* Princeton: Princeton University Press.

de Tocqueville, A. (1990) [1835/1840]. *Democracy in America* (Vol. I). New York: Vintage Books.

Drent, M., & Meijnders, M. (2015, September). *Multi-year Defence Agreements: A Model for Modern Defence?* Clingendael Report. The Hague: Netherlands Institute of International Relations.

Eichbaum, C., & Shaw, R. (2014). Prime Ministers and Their Advisers in Parliamentary Democracies. In R. A. W. Rhodes & P. 't Hart (Eds.), *The Oxford Handbook of Political Leadership* (pp. 517–531). Oxford: Oxford University Press.

Elgie, R. (2001). Cohabitation: Divided Government French-Style. In R. Elgie (Ed.), *Divided Government in Comparative Perspective* (pp. 106–126). Oxford: Oxford University Press.

Elgie, R. (2018). List of Cohabitations. The Semi-Presidential One. Blog Post by Robert Elgie. www.semipresidentialism.com. Accessed 7 Oct 2018.

Finnemore, M. (1996). *National Interests in International Society.* Ithaca: Cornell University Press.

Gherghina, S., & Kopecký, P. (Eds.). (2016). Politicization of Administrative Elites in Western Europe. *Acta Politica, 51*(4), 407–412.

Gilmour, J. B. (2002). Institutional and Individual Influences on the President's Veto. *The Journal of Politics, 64*(1), 198–218.

Goldmann, K. (2005). Appropriateness and Consequences: The Logic of Neo-Institutionalism. *Governance, 18*(1), 35–52.

Goodin, R. E. (Ed.). (1996). *The Theory of Institutional Design.* Cambridge: Cambridge University Press.

Greif, A., & Kingston, C. (2011). Institutions: Rules or Equilibria? In N. Schofield & G. Caballero (Eds.), *Political Economy of Institutions, Democracy and Voting* (pp. 13–44). Berlin: Springer.

Hager, G. L., & Sullivan, T. (1994). President-Centered and Presidency-Centered Explanations of Presidential Public Activity. *American Journal of Political Science, 38*(4), 1079–1103.

Hall, P. A., & Taylor, R. C. R. (1996). Political Science and the Three New Institutionalisms. *Political Studies, 44*(5), 936–957.

Hegeland, H. (2007). The European Union in National Parliaments: Domestic or Foreign Policy? A Study of Nordic Parliamentary Systems. In J. O'Brennan & T. Raunio (Eds.), *National Parliaments Within the Enlarged European Union: From 'Victims' of Integration to Competitive Actors?* (pp. 95–115). London: Routledge.

Helmke, G., & Levitsky, S. (2004). Informal Institutions and Comparative Politics: A Research Agenda. *Perspectives on Politics, 2*(4), 725–740.

Helmke, G., & Levitsky, S. (2006a). Conclusion. In G. Helmke & S. Levitsky (Eds.), *Informal Institutions & Democracy: Lessons from Latin America* (pp. 274–284). Baltimore: The Johns Hopkins University Press.

Helmke, G., & Levitsky, S. (2006b). Introduction. In G. Helmke & S. Levitsky (Eds.), *Informal Institutions & Democracy: Lessons from Latin America* (pp. 1–30). Baltimore: The Johns Hopkins University Press.

Helms, L. (Ed.). (2012). *Comparative Political Leadership*. Basingstoke: Palgrave Macmillan.

Hill, C. (2013). *The National Interest in Question: Foreign Policy in Multicultural Societies*. Oxford: Oxford University Press.

Howell, W. G., Jackman, S. P., & Rogowski, J. C. (2013). *The Wartime President: Executive Influence and the Nationalizing Politics of Threat*. Chicago: The University of Chicago Press.

Kassim, H., Guy Peters, B., & Wright, V. (Eds.). (2000). *The National Co-ordination of EU Policy: The Domestic Level*. Oxford: Oxford University Press.

Kernell, S. (2007). *Going Public: New Strategies of Presidential Leadership* (4th ed.). Washington, DC: CQ Press.

Köker, P. (2017). *Presidential Activism and Veto Power in Central and Eastern Europe*. Cham: Palgrave Macmillan.

Lauth, H.-J. (2000). Informal Institutions and Democracy. *Democratization, 7*(4), 21–50.

Lauth, H.-J. (2015). Formal and Informal Institutions. In J. Gandhi & R. Ruiz-Rufino (Eds.), *Routledge Handbook of Comparative Political Institutions* (pp. 56–69). London: Routledge.

Lazardeux, S. G. (2015). *Cohabitation and Conflicting Politics in French Policymaking*. Basingstoke: Palgrave Macmillan.

Leuffen, D. (2009). Does Cohabitation Matter? French European Policy-Making in the Context of Divided Government. *West European Politics, 32*(6), 1140–1160.

Locke, J. (1960) [1690]. *Two Treatises of Government*. Cambridge: Cambridge University Press.

Lowndes, V., & Roberts, M. (2013). *Why Institutions Matter: The New Institutionalism in Political Science*. Basingstoke: Palgrave Macmillan.

March, J. G., & Olsen, J. P. (1989). *Rediscovering Institutions: The Organizational Basis of Politics*. New York: The Free Press.

March, J. G., & Olsen, J. P. (2004). *The Logic of Appropriateness* (Arena Working Paper 04/09). Oslo.

March, J. G., & Olsen, J. P. (2006). The Logic of Appropriateness. In M. Moran, M. Rein, & R. E. Goodin (Eds.), *The Oxford Handbook of Public Policy* (pp. 689–708). Oxford: Oxford University Press.

Marland, A., Lewis, J. P., & Flanagan, T. (2017). Governance in the Age of Digital Media and Branding. *Governance: An International Journal of Policy, Administration and Institutions, 30*(1), 125–141.

Messick, D. M. (1999). Alternative Logics for Decision Making in Social Settings. *Journal of Economic Behavior and Organization, 39*(1), 11–28.

Milner, H. V., & Tingley, D. (2015). *Sailing the Water's Edge: The Domestic Politics of American Foreign Policy*. Princeton: Princeton University Press.

Mitchell, D. (2005). Centralizing Advisory Systems: Presidential Influence and the U.S. Foreign Policy Decision-Making Process. *Foreign Policy Analysis, 1*(2), 181–206.

Mueller, J. E. (1973). *War, Presidents, and Public Opinion*. New York: Wiley.

Müller, W. C., & Strøm, K. (Eds.). (1999). *Policy, Office, or Votes? How Political Parties in Western Europe Make Hard Decisions*. Cambridge: Cambridge University Press.

Müller, W. C., & Strøm, K. (Eds.). (2000). *Coalition Governments in Western Europe*. Oxford: Oxford University Press.

North, D. C. (1990). *Institutions, Institutional Change and Economic Performance*. Cambridge: Cambridge University Press.

North, D. C. (1993). Institutions and Credible Commitment. *Journal of Institutional and Theoretical Economics, 149*(1), 11–23.

O'Neal, J. R., Lian, B., & Joyner, J. H., Jr. (1996). Are the American People "Pretty Prudent"? Public Responses to U.S. Uses of Force, 1950–1988. *International Studies Quarterly, 40*(2), 261–279.

Passarelli, G. (Ed.). (2015). *The Presidentialization of Political Parties: Organizations, Institutions and Leaders*. Basingstoke: Palgrave Macmillan.

Pierson, P. (2000). Increasing Returns, Path Dependence, and the Study of Politics. *American Political Science Review, 94*(2), 251–267.

Raunio, T. (2012). Semi-Presidentialism and European Integration: Lessons from Finland for Constitutional Design. *Journal of European Public Policy, 19*(4), 567–584.

Raunio, T. (2016). Refusing to Be Sidelined: The Engagement of the Finnish Eduskunta in Foreign Affairs. *Scandinavian Political Studies, 39*(4), 312–332.

Raunio, T., & Wagner, W. (2017). Towards Parliamentarization of Foreign and Security Policy? *West European Politics, 40*(1), 1–19.

Rhodes, R. A. W., & 't Hart, P. (Eds.). (2014). *The Oxford Handbook of Political Leadership*. Oxford: Oxford University Press.

Rhodes, R. A. W., Binder, S. A., & Rockman, B. A. (Eds.). (2006). *The Oxford Handbook of Political Institutions*. Oxford: Oxford University Press.

Riggs, F. W. (1988). The Survival of Presidentialism in America: Para-Constitutional Practices. *International Political Science Review, 9*(4), 247–278.

Rosenau, J. N. (1971). *The Scientific Study of Foreign Policy*. New York: The Free Press.

Samuels, D. J., & Shugart, M. S. (2010). *Presidents, Parties, and Prime Ministers: How the Separation of Powers Affects Party Organization and Behavior*. Cambridge: Cambridge University Press.

Scharpf, F. W. (1989). Decision Rules, Decision Styles and Policy Choices. *Journal of Theoretical Politics, 1*(2), 149–176.

Scott, W. R. (2014). *Institutions and Organizations: Ideas, Interests, and Identities* (4th ed.). London: Sage.

Siavelis, P. (2006). Accommodating Informal Institutions and Chilean Democracy. In G. Helmke & S. Levitsky (Eds.), *Informal Institutions & Democracy: Lessons from Latin America* (pp. 33–55). Baltimore: The Johns Hopkins University Press.

Strøm, K. (1990). A Behavioral Theory of Competitive Political Parties. *American Journal of Political Science, 34*(2), 565–598.

Strøm, K., Müller, W. C., & Bergman, T. (Eds.). (2008). *Cabinets and Coalition Bargaining: The Democratic Life Cycle in Western Europe*. Oxford: Oxford University Press.

Tavits, M. (2009). *Presidents with Prime Ministers: Do Direct Elections Matter?* Oxford: Oxford University Press.

Thelen, K. (1999). Historical Institutionalism in Comparative Politics. *Annual Review of Political Science, 2*, 369–404.

Waever, O. (1995). Securitization and Desecuritization. In R. D. Lipschutz (Ed.), *On Security* (pp. 46–86). New York: Columbia University Press.

Weaver, R. K., & Rockman, B. A. (Eds.). (1993). *Do Institutions Matter? Government Capabilities in the United States and Abroad*. Washington, DC: The Brookings Institution.

Yong, B., & Hazell, R. (2014). *Special Advisers: Who They Are, What They Do and Why They Matter*. Oxford: Hart Publishing.

CHAPTER 3

The Semi-Presidential Cases in Comparative Context

This chapter sets Finland, Lithuania, and Romania in a comparative context of semi-presidentialism in Europe. The aim is twofold: first to place and justify the selection of our three cases by including them in a wider set of semi-presidential regimes, and second to use this wider comparison to provide a range of basic and institutional data for setting the stage of the subsequent chapters on executive coordination. We provide key data on semi-presidential subtypes (premier-presidentialism and president-parliamentarism), level of democracy, dimensions of presidential power, intra-executive conflict, and cohabitation. Our presentation is inevitably kept on a general and comparative level but gives empirical prominence to our three cases. In a separate section, we also assess, by the use of public opinion data, general levels of institutional trust with an emphasis on public support for the presidency. Finally, we conclude the chapter by summarizing the argument for our case selection and focused comparison.

3.1   Semi-Presidential Regimes in Europe

Table 3.1 reports on basic constitutional and political indicators in 16 premier-presidential and four president-parliamentary regimes in Europe. Semi-presidentialism, in either of its two main forms, is currently the most common constitutional arrangement in Europe. One may immediately object to such a list of semi-presidential regimes on the basis that it includes countries that are unequivocally autocracies

© The Author(s) 2020   45
T. Raunio, T. Sedelius, *Semi-Presidential Policy-Making in Europe*,
Palgrave Studies in Presidential Politics,
https://doi.org/10.1007/978-3-030-16431-7_3

Table 3.1   Comparative indicators on semi-presidential countries in Europe

Country	Year of semi-presidential constitution	Democracy 2018 Freedom in the world aggregate scores	EU member Y/N (year of membership)	Electoral system, lower house
Premier-presidential				
Bulgaria	1991	80/100 (F)	Y (2007)	PR-list
Croatia	2001	86/100 (F)	Y (2013)	PR-list
Czech Republic	2012	93/100 (F)	Y (2004)	PR-list
Finland	1919	100/100 (F)	Y (1995)	PR-list
France	1962	90/100 (F)	Y (1958)	TRS
Ireland	1937	96/100 (F)	Y (1973)	STV
Lithuania	1992	91/100 (F)	Y (2004)	Parallel
Macedonia	1991	58/100 (PF)	N	PR-list
Moldova	1994, 2016	61/100 (PF)	N	PR-list
Montenegro	2007	67/100 (PF)	N	PR-list
Poland	1997	85/100 (F)	Y (2004)	PR-list
Romania	1991	84/100 (F)	Y (2007)	PR-list
Serbia	2006	74/100 (F)	N	PR-list
Slovakia	1999	89/100 (F)	Y (2004)	PR-list
Slovenia	1991	93/100 (F)	Y (2004)	PR-list
Ukraine	2006, 2014	62/100 (PF)	N	Parallel
President-parliamentary				
Austria	1929	94/100 (F)	Y (1995)	PR-list
Belarus	1996	21/100 (NF)	N	TRS
Iceland	1944	95/100 (F)	N	PR-list
Russia	1993-	20/100 (NF)	N	Parallel

Notes and abbreviations: Freedom House annually measures civil liberties and political rights and provides an aggregated "Freedom Score" from 0 (least free) to 100 (most free). *F* free, *PF* partly free, *NF* not free, *PR-list* proportional representation, party-list system, *STV* single transferable vote, *TRS* two round system, *Parallel* mixed system, PR + First Past the Post
Source: Freedom in the World (2018), List of Electoral Systems by Country (2018), Wikipedia

such as Belarus and Russia, and that it includes countries with very weak presidencies that are often classified by other scholars as parliamentary, such as Ireland, Iceland, and Slovenia. Yet, when using the conventional constitutional criteria of semi-presidentialism and its two subtypes, premier-presidentialism and president-parliamentarism, these countries qualify all the same. We will not repeat here the argument from Chap. 1 for why we should stick to purely constitutional definitions when categorizing regime types. However, an essential part of any classification of semi-presidentialism is also to carefully attend to dimensions and measures of presidential power, which we will do in the next section. First, we make some general observations on the European pattern of semi-presidentialism.

Among the established democracies in Europe, Austria and Iceland are indeed exceptional having president-parliamentary constitutions. An obvious reason why their president-parliamentary constitutions are somewhat overlooked in the comparative literature is that they have functioned under highly 'parliamentarized' political systems where the president's de facto role has been very limited. Similarly, although under a premier-presidential constitution with a formally weak presidency, Ireland has experienced marginal intervention by the president in executive politics.

Ever since Duverger originally coined the concept, Finland and France are standard reference cases of semi-presidentialism. This is due to the fact that they are the most long-term established and uninterrupted semi-presidential democracies. As one of our three selected cases, we examine Finland's constitutional system in more detail below. For more comprehensive works (in English) on semi-presidentialism in the French Fifth Republic, see, for example, Bell (2000), Bell and Gaffney (2013), and Lazardeux (2015).

In addition to Finland, France, and Ireland, premier-presidential constitutions are widespread among the post-communist countries in Central Europe, whereas president-parliamentary constitutions are in place in Austria and Iceland and in the authoritarian post-Soviet regimes of Belarus and Russia. President-parliamentary constitutions were originally installed in many post-Soviet countries in and outside of Eastern Europe, including in Armenia (1995–2005), Azerbaijan (1995–), Belarus (1994–), Georgia (1995–2013), Kyrgyzstan (1993–2007), Ukraine (1996–2005, 2010–2014), and Russia (1993–), but only three of these countries are left with this form of constitution in 2018—Azerbaijan, Belarus, and Russia. Notably, the latter have been headed by authoritarian presidents, where constitutional amendments were adopted to strengthen already powerful presidencies. In the opposite direction, Armenia, Croatia (2001–), Georgia, and Ukraine represent constitutional change away from a president-dominated system toward premier-presidentialism, where the cabinet is exclusively dependent on the parliament for survival.

Obviously, constitutional choice is a complex phenomenon and includes a varying mix of actor-oriented, historical-institutional, critical juncture effects, and diffusion components that are not easily disentangled (cf. Jung and Deering 2015; Lijphart and Waisman 2006;

Åberg and Denk 2019) and are well beyond the focus of this study. Yet, a general pattern separating the Central European countries from the (non-Baltic) post-Soviet context is the way in which the transition played out in 1989–1991. Central Europe experienced a post-communist transition more characterized by bottom-up revolutions than was the case in the post-Soviet republics, where the transition was primarily led by top-level elites from the previous regime. There were negotiations involving parties or popular movements, not just individual actors; and consequently, constitutional reform was not directed by the president to the same extent as in many former Soviet republics. This is not to say that the presidents were absent from the constitutional process, but that they played a different and less prominent role. This factor, together with historical-geographical and political-cultural dimensions such as the close ties of these countries to the West European sphere where parliamentary constitutions are predominant, helps to understand why presidential-parliamentary and presidential constitutions were rejected in favor of models in which the government is anchored in the parliament—parliamentarism and premier-presidentialism (Sedelius 2008).

Although the semi-presidential concept was originally coined by Duverger and very much centered on the French Fifth Republic, Finland was an earlier adopter of the regime type. In the wake of independence in 1919, following a civil war, the former monarchists on the right (the Whites) favored a president-dominated system whereas the former Reds in the Social Democratic camp advocated a parliament-based model. Ultimately, the Constitutional Committee came up with a compromise where the president would acquire significant powers and be elected by an electoral college following a popular vote. Apparently, the Finnish republican constitution of 1919 displayed certain elements from a monarchist tradition, where the president assumed powers of the former Czar, including the direction of foreign policy and dissolution of the Eduskunta (parliament). Both the former monarchists and the White republicans considered a strong president necessary as a counterweight to a leftist-dominated parliament.

The semi-presidential constitution in Lithuania was a compromise with the intention of combining the prospects of legitimacy derived from the parliament with a dual executive structure. A premier-presidential constitution was adopted in 1992 under the post-Soviet context of deep ideological cleavages, weak parties, and personally based politics. To some extent, inter-war experiences of powerful presidencies influenced the establishment of a popularly elected president. There were connotations made to the inter-war period when the constitutional order was characterized by a strong presidency channeled through the national figure Antanas Smetona. Smetona is regarded in the Lithuanian society as a leader who created a strong independent state and there was a desire to restore such images of stability and national pride. Although the main political groups rejected the idea of just copying the undemocratic 1938 constitution, demands for a strong presidency prevailed—especially within the popular front movement, *Sajūdis*, and its leader, Vytautas Landsbergis. *Sajūdis* even leaned toward presidentialism, envisioning a president in charge of government and with the right to appoint and dismiss cabinets without parliamentary support. However, the former communists in the Democratic Labour Party of Lithuania (LDDP), who initially outlined a pure parliamentary system, strongly opposed such proposals, and as a result, the final draft represented a compromise between these two rival forces (Holm-Hansen 2006; Nørgaard and Johannsen 1999).

In Romania, there was relatively little debate on the institutional provisions of the constitution during the drafting process. In this respect Romania was rather different from other semi-presidential countries in Central and Eastern Europe. This was due in part to the riots in Bucharest in September 1991 and the subsequent intra-executive conflict between President Iliescu and Prime Minister Roman, which preoccupied Romanian politics at that time. For another part, the relative lack of constitutional debate can be explained by the dominant position of the left-wing National Salvation Front (NSF), which gave other political parties little influence over the constitution-building process. In contrast to Lithuania, there was no clear precedent for the development of a semi-presidential system in Romania, and it is difficult to find historical-institutional determinants, although one could argue that also in this case a strongman tradition was constitutionalized. The close relations between Romania and France can provide a partial explanation. The constitution reflects the French one in many ways. In addition to the semi-presidential features of executive-legislative relations, the design of institutional relations between local and central government is very close to the French system, as well as the set-up of a bicameral system.

Table 3.1 also provides an overview of the 2018 aggregated Freedom House scores based on civil liberties and political rights, which is a rough but frequently used measure of the level of democracy. With the exception of the full-fledged autocracies with president-parliamentary constitutions, Belarus and Russia (both classified as Not Free)—the semi-presidential countries are classified as Partly Free in four cases (Macedonia, Moldova, Montenegro, and Ukraine), and Free in the remaining 14 cases. Among the countries denoted as Free there is some notable variation on the aggregated scores, where only Finland comes out with the maximum 100, followed by a group of countries above 90 (Austria, Iceland, the Czech Republic, France, Ireland, Lithuania, and Slovenia) and a subsequent group of countries in the range of 80–89 (Bulgaria, Croatia, Poland, Romania, and Slovakia). Finally, Serbia just barely reaches the 'Free' status with an aggregated score of 74. Iceland and Serbia aside, these countries are all EU members with Croatia as the most recent candidate to join in 2013.

The last column in Table 3.1 reports on electoral systems for the parliament's lower house. As can be seen, most of the premier-presidential countries operate with party-list proportional elections. Among the democracies these exceptions are France using a majority-based Two Round System, Ireland using a preferential and highly proportional Single Transferable Vote System, and Lithuania using a parallel (Proportional Representation and First Past the Post combined) system. Thus, for our focused comparison, we should keep in mind that Lithuania differs from Finland and Romania in this regard, where the plurality component of the parallel electoral system expectedly reduces the number of parliamentary parties.

Overall, our three selected cases of European premier-presidentialism have democracy scores that are sufficient to place them in the 'Free' category but with varying degrees. Finland, as a long-established and prosperous democracy in Scandinavia, continuously ranks at the very top level in various democracy rankings including in Freedom House. Post-Soviet Lithuania, as a much younger democracy, has performance scores that are overall stronger than for Romania, which was also confirmed by Lithuania's earlier membership in the EU (2004)—three years ahead of Romania (2007). The more struggling path to democracy in Romania is further illustrated by the subcategories in Freedom House's *Nations in Transit* reported in Table 3.2 (Finland not included). The scores are the Freedom House standard scale, where 1 is 'most free' and 7 is 'least free'. Romania's scores are systematically below Lithuania for all categories and throughout the whole reported period 2010–2018. In fact, Romania fares relatively

Table 3.2 Nations in Transit 2010–2018, ratings and average scores: Lithuania and Romania

Nations in Transit	2010	2011	2012	2013	2014	2015	2016	2017	2018
National democratic governance									
Lithuania	2.75	2.75	2.75	2.75	2.75	2.75	2.75	2.75	2.75
Romania	4.00	3.75	3.75	4.00	3.75	3.75	3.75	3.50	3.75
Electoral process									
Lithuania	1.75	1.75	1.75	2.00	2.00	2.00	2.00	2.00	2.00
Romania	2.75	2.75	3.00	3.00	3.00	3.25	3.25	3.00	3.00
Civil society									
Lithuania	1.75	1.75	1.75	1.75	1.75	1.75	1.75	1.75	2.00
Romania	2.50	2.50	2.50	2.50	2.50	2.50	2.25	2.25	2.25
Independent media									
Lithuania	1.75	1.75	2.00	2.00	2.25	2.25	2.25	2.25	2.25
Romania	4.00	4.00	4.00	4.25	4.25	4.25	4.25	4.25	4.25
Local democratic governance									
Lithuania	2.50	2.50	2.50	2.50	2.50	2.50	2.25	2.25	2.25
Romania	3.00	3.00	3.00	3.00	3.00	3.00	3.25	3.25	3.50
Judicial framework and independence									
Lithuania	1.75	1.75	1.75	1.75	1.75	1.75	1.75	1.75	1.75
Romania	4.00	4.00	3.75	3.75	3.75	3.75	3.75	3.75	3.75
Corruption									
Lithuania	3.50	3.50	3.50	3.50	3.50	3.50	3.50	3.50	3.50
Romania	4.00	4.00	4.00	4.00	4.00	3.75	3.75	3.75	3.75
Overall democracy score									
Lithuania	2.25	2.25	2.29	2.32	2.36	2.36	2.32	2.32	2.36
Romania	3.46	3.43	3.43	3.50	3.46	3.46	3.46	3.39	3.46

Note: Aggregated scores are based on the Freedom House standard scale, where 1 is 'most free' and 7 is 'least free'
Source: Nations in Transit 2018, www.freedomhouse.org

poor on Democratic Governance (3.75, 2018), Independent Media (4.25), Judicial Framework and Independence (3.75), and Corruption (3.75). Notably, in their overall assessment in 2018, *Nations in Transit* classify Romania as a 'semi-consolidated democracy' and Lithuania as a 'consolidated democracy'.

Similar to the democracy rankings, Finland is among the countries in the world with the lowest levels of corruption. In Transparency International's Corruption Perception Index (CPI) 2017 including 180 countries, Finland ranks as number 3, Lithuania as number 38, and Romania as number 59.

3.2   PRESIDENTIAL POWER

Comparative analyses of semi-presidentialism need to take into account the powers provided to the president. Ever since Duverger (1980: 161) introduced the criterion of semi-presidentialism that the "president possess quite considerable powers", this has been a matter of debate. The now widely used definition by Elgie (1999) removes any references to presidential powers and therefore yields a very diverse set of semi-presidential countries. Shugart and Carey's (1992) subtypes of premier-presidentialism and president-parliamentarism help to reduce this heterogeneity, but still generate two categories with considerable variation on presidential power. Fortunately, there are now many existing measures of presidential powers available in the literature—all with benefits and shortcomings. Here we report on three variants that we believe provide both general and some more detailed information.

Table 3.3 provides presidential power scores as reported by Doyle and Elgie (2016). The main advantage of these scores is that they are compiled and weighted based on 28 already existing measures in the literature. In addition, Doyle and Elgie have generated their dataset on a larger number of countries with longer time series than any other existing measure. The scores are in the range from 0 (lowest) to 1 (highest) in separate time periods following constitutional changes of a country's presidential powers.

The average presidential power scores confirm an expected pattern where the premier-presidential countries score considerably lower (0.197) than the president-parliamentary countries (0.399). Our limited sample of post-communist countries also testify to a more general pattern where the East European and post-Soviet countries with the strongest presidential powers are also the ones with the worst records of democratization. In Table 3.3 this includes Belarus, Russia, and Ukraine (1996–2006, 2010–2014). Indeed, in Belarus and Russia, the strong presidential component, introduced from the outset of independence, has contributed to legitimize and reinforce authoritarian tendencies.

Leaving the president-parliamentary cases aside, the premier-presidential countries are arranged from lowest to highest, where we find Finland's post-2000 constitution to provide the weakest presidential powers (0.050) of all the listed cases on this measure. On almost the opposite end, the presidencies in Romania (0.250) and Lithuania (0.282) receive relatively high scores within the premier-presidential category. This is, however, somewhat nuanced when we turn to two more detailed presidential power measures.

Table 3.3 Doyle and Elgie's presidential power scores in European semi-presidential countries

Constitutional type	Country	Presidential power Doyle and Elgie (2016), Prespower1 Normalized score (standard error) year interval
Premier-presidential	Finland	**0.050 (0.035) 2000–**
	Ireland	0.062 (0.048) 1938–
	Slovenia	0.118 (0.019) 1992–
	France	0.131 (0.020) 1963–
	Bulgaria	0.183 (0.044) 1992–
	Slovakia	0.189 (0.139) 2002–
	Portugal	0.197 (0.016) 1983–
	Moldova	0.240 (0.059) 1995–2000
	Poland	0.241 (0.044) 1997–
	Romania	**0.250 (0.033) 1992–**
	Lithuania	**0.282 (0.044) 1993–**
	Croatia 2001–	0.291 (0.074) 2001–
	Ukraine 2005–2010, 2014–	0.329 (0.206) 2005–2010
Average score		0.197
President-parliamentary	Austria	0.092 (0.012) 1945–
	Iceland	0.325 (0.079) 1944–
	Croatia 1991–2000	0.335 (0.050) 1991–2000
	Ukraine 1996–2005, 2010–2014	0.464 (0.065) 2011–2014 0.440 (0.061) 1996–2004
	Russia	0.561 (0.056) 1994–
	Belarus	0.615 (0.094) 1997–
Average score		0.399

Note: Countries arranged in order of presidential power scores. Doyle and Elgie have developed two sets of scores, Prespower1 and Prespower2, and there are some differences in statistical specifications behind the two. In terms of standard errors for the European countries, however, there are similar and acceptable ranges and we report only the Prespower1 scores here
Sources: Doyle and Elgie (2016), Elgie (2015)

Table 3.4 reports on the long-standing and most widely cited measure of presidential power developed by Shugart and Carey (1992). They separate between six 'legislative' and four 'non-legislative' powers with a minimum score of 0 to maximum 4 on each power. The measure confirms that premier-presidentialism in Europe provides, in general, for relatively weak presidencies and again that Finland's post-2000 constitution belongs to the group where formal powers of the president are few indeed. Even here, Lithuania and Romania score higher than Finland on both legislative

Table 3.4 Shugart and Carey's presidential power scores in European semi-presidential countries

	PKV	PTV	DC	EXL	BUD	REF	CF	CD	CEN	DIS	TOT
Premier-presidentialism											
Ireland	0	0	0	0	0	0	0	0	0	0	0
Finland	0	0	1	0	0	0	0	0	0	0	1
Macedonia	1	0	0	0	0	0	1	0	0	0	2
Bulgaria	1	0	1	0	0	0	0	0	0	0	2
Slovakia 1999–	1	0	0	0	0	0	1	0	0	1	3
Slovenia	0	0	1	0	0	0	1	0	1	1	4
France	0	1	0	0	0	0	1	0	0	3	5
Lithuania	1	0	1	0	0	0	1	0	2	1	6
Poland	1	0	0	0	0	2	1	0	1	1	6
Ukraine 2006–10, 2014–	2	0	1	0	0	2	0	0	0	1	6
Moldova 1991–2000, 2016–	0	0	1	0	0	4	1	0	0	1	7
Croatia 2001–	0	0	1	0	0	2	1	0	2	1	7
Romania	0	0	1	0	0	4	1	0	0	1	7
Portugal	2	0	0	0	0	0	1	2	0	3	8
President-parliamentarism											
Austria	0	0	0	0	0	0	1	0	0	3	4
Croatia 1990–2001	0	0	1	0	0	2	1	2	2	1	9
Iceland	0	0	1	0	0	2	4	0	0	4	11
Ukraine 1996–2006, 2010–2014	2	0	4	0	0	2	1	4	0	0	13
Russia 1993–	2	0	4	0	0	1	4	2	1	0	14
Belarus 1997–	2	0	4	0	0	4	3	2	4	0	19

Note: Countries arranged in order of total scores. Shugart and Carey's measure of presidential power separates between six legislative powers (*PKV* package veto, *PTV* pocket veto, *DC* decree powers, *EXL* exclusive initiative of legislation, *BUD* budgetary powers, *REF* referendum initiative) and four non-legislative powers (*CF* cabinet formation, *CD* cabinet dismissal, *CEN* cabinet censure, *DIS* dissolution of assembly). Each power is scored from 0 to 4, with a total maximum power score of 40 altogether. For a full explanation of the scoring scheme, see Shugart and Carey (1992: 148–152)
Source: Adapted from Shugart and Carey (1992), Elgie (2010), Elgie and Moestrup (2008)

and non-legislative powers. Restricted but observable presidential powers in Lithuania are distributed across five categories—package veto, decree power, cabinet formation, cabinet censure, and dissolution of parliament. The 1-point higher total score in Romania is distributed across four of the included categories—decree power, referenda initiative, cabinet formation, and dissolution of parliament.

An alternative to Shugart and Carey's measure is developed by Siaroff (2003). He provides a partly different set of categories including, for example, concurrent presidential and parliamentary elections (CE), whether the president chairs cabinet meetings (CM), has a central role in foreign policy (FP), and has a central role in government formation (GF). The country scores are dichotomous 0 (No) and 1 (Yes) and are collected from Siaroff's own study. We believe that this either-or (0 or 1) measure somewhat underestimates presidential powers. For example, in most semi-presidential countries, including in Finland (Article 93), the president has an assigned constitutional role in foreign policy, which Siaroff's measure does not capture. However, these data (Table 3.5) generate a similar overview as for

Table 3.5 Siaroff's presidential power scores in European semi-presidential countries

	CE	AP	CM	VT	EDP	FP	GF	DL	TOT
Premier-presidentialism									
Slovenia	0	0	0	0	0	0	0	0	0
Finland	0	0	0	1	0	0	0	0	**1**
Slovakia 1999–	0	0	0	1	0	0	0	0	1
Ireland	0	1	0	1	0	0	0	0	2
Bulgaria	0	1	0	1	0	0	0	0	2
Poland	0	1	0	1	0	0	0	0	2
Portugal	0	0	0	1	0	0	0	1	2
Macedonia	0	1	0	1	0	1	0	0	3
Lithuania	0	1	0	1	0	1	0	0	**3**
Croatia 2001–	0	1	1	0	1	0	0	0	3
Moldova 1991–2000, 2016–	0	1	1	1	0	1	0	0	4
Romania	1	1	1	1	0	0	0	0	**4**
France	0	1	1	1	0	1	1	1	6
President-parliamentarism									
Austria	0	0	0	0	0	0	0	0	0
Iceland	0	0	0	0	0	0	0	0	0
Croatia 1990–2001	0	1	1	0	1	1	1	0	5
Russia	0	1	1	1	1	1	1	0	6
Belarus 1994–1996	0	1	1	1	1	1	1	0	6
Ukraine 1996–2006, 2010–2014	0	1	1	1	1	1	1	0	7

Note: Countries arranged in order of total scores. Siaroff's measure of presidential power separates between *CE* concurrent presidential and legislative elections, *AP* discretionary appointment powers, *CM* chairing of cabinet meetings, *VT* right to veto, *EDP* long-term emergency and/or decree powers, *FP* central role in foreign policy, *GF* central role in foreign policy, *DL* ability to dissolve the legislature. Each power is scored 0 (no) or 1 (yes). Siaroff's measure also includes whether the president is popularly elected. This category is excluded here as popular election of the president is a (semi-presidential) criterion for the listed countries. For a full explanation of the scoring scheme, see Siaroff (2003: 303–308). No data provided on Ukraine 2006–2010
Source: Adapted from Siaroff (2003)

Shugart and Carey's measure. Finland ends up in the group of semi-presidential countries with the weakest presidency, whereas Lithuania and, even more so, Romania belong to a semi-presidential group in Europe with medium-strong presidencies. Apparently, the Romanian constitution resembles the French Fifth Republic also on presidential powers. Nevertheless, the Romanian constitution provides more restricted powers in some notable respects. Strict limitations on the presidential power to dissolve the parliament and the fact that the parliament has to approve the use of decree powers by the executive are important deviations from the Fifth Republic's system. These deviations were a reaction to the abuse of the unlimited powers granted to the communist dictator Nicolae Ceausescu under the communist institutional system (Sedelius 2006: 107–108).

Despite their limited legislative and policy powers, the presidents perform a number of representative functions and are constitutionally assigned with a political voice in national security and foreign affairs. Finland's constitution recognizes in Article 93 that "the foreign policy of Finland is directed by the President [...] in co-operation with the Government". However, "the Parliament accepts Finland's international obligations and their denouncement and decides on the bringing into force of Finland's international obligations in so far as provided in this Constitution". Similarly, the wording of the Lithuanian constitution is that the president "shall decide the basic issues of foreign policy and, together with the Government, conduct foreign policy" (Article 84:1). In the same way, Article 80:1 in the Romanian constitution declares that the president "shall represent the Romanian State and is the safeguard of the national independence, unity and territorial integrity of the country". In the same article (80:2), the president is figuratively assigned "to guard the observance of the Constitution and the proper functioning of the public authorities" and to "act as a mediator between the Powers in the State as well as between the State and society". In addition, the presidents in all three countries have a set of appointment powers to high-level offices and public administration. Usually these are shared with the prime minister or other bodies and include, for example, the right to nominate judges to the Constitutional Court, the Chairman of the National Bank, the Commander of the Army, the Head of the Security Service, and the Prosecutor General.

Before leaving this comparative overview on presidential power, there are reasons to look a bit more closely on Finland. As indicated in the reported power measures, the Finnish president has, according to the 2000 constitution, very limited authority in government formation and dissolution matters, decision-making, and decree and veto powers. However, as can be seen in Table 3.6, before 2000 the president's formal powers were significantly stronger. Indeed, both the Doyle and Elgie measure and Siaroff's scores would place pre-2000 Finland among the premier-presidential countries with the overall strongest presidencies. Section 2 of the 1919 Constitutional Act stated that "Legislative power should be exercised by Parliament in conjunction with the President of the Republic. Supreme executive power should be vested in the President of the Republic." Until 1991, the president had the unilateral right—without even consulting the cabinet or the parliament—to dissolve the parliament and call early elections. A 1991 amendment to the constitution weakened the president's power in this regard by requiring explicit consent by the prime minister for dissolving the parliament.

At least until the 1980s, Finland's semi-presidential system was characterized by salient and powerful figures like President Urho Kekkonen and President Mauno Koivisto. Especially Kekkonen took on a strong executive role in managing the country's sensitive relations with the Soviet Union, which made him at times an omnipresent leader on the political scene in Finland. During the Kekkonen era, the political system became increasingly president dominated as a direct consequence of the sensitive Finnish-Soviet relations and the style of personal leadership developed by Kekkonen himself. The geo-political location of Finland under the Cold War forced the Finnish leaders to maintain good relations with Moscow following two defeats by the Red Army between 1939 and 1944. However, when the Soviet Union collapsed, so too did one of the foundations of presidential power, which made possible a shift toward a significantly more parliamentarized political system. The country's membership in the European Union in 1995 further strengthened the role of the prime minister (Anckar 1999; Arter 1999; Paloheimo 2001).

Table 3.6 Presidential power scores, Finland 1919–2018

Finland	Doyle and Elgie	Siaroff								
Years		CE	AP	CM	VT	EDP	FP	GF	DL	TOT
1919–1956	–	0	1	1	1	0	1	0	0	4
1957–1994	0.157	0	1	1	1	0	1	1	0	5
1995–1999	0.162	0	1	1	1	0	1	0	0	4
2000–	0.050	0	1	0	1	0	0	0	0	2

Note: See Tables 3.3 and 3.5
Source: Adapted from Doyle and Elgie (2016), Siaroff (2003)

Finland is thus a case of a constitutionally weak presidency embedded in a heritage of formally and informally strong presidents. In the subsequent empirical chapters, we are interested in the extent to which such institutional legacies impact on coordination and power-sharing between the president and the government.

3.3   PRESIDENT-CABINET CONFLICT AND COHABITATION

In our study, we are interested in exploring how executive coordination matters to executive power-sharing between the president and the prime minister. One obvious way to assess power-sharing status within the executive is to tap into the frequency of intra-executive conflict—that is, to assess instances of severe and persistent tensions between the president and the cabinet. Premier-presidential systems are expected to generate instances of intra-executive conflict because only the parliament and not the president can dismiss the prime minister. As the cabinet is dependent on parliamentary support for claiming authority to control the executive branch, its political orientation is likely to ultimately steer in favor of the parliamentary majority. In other words, where the president and the parliamentary majority do not find common ground, the prime minister is expected to side with the parliament rather than with the president (Protsyk 2005, 2006; Sedelius and Ekman 2010; Shugart and Carey 1992). As such, conflicts between the president and the cabinet over appointments, dismissals, policy, and constitutional rules are manifestations of the institutional competition embedded into the dual executive structure of semi-presidentialism. Still, we find no clear evidence in the literature that intra-executive conflict by itself has caused regime breakdown, although it has clearly been an involved factor in severe constitutional struggles, for example, in Romania and Ukraine. Different studies have reported on the frequency of intra-executive conflict in semi-presidential countries. Sedelius and Mashtaler (2013) showed that intra-executive conflict occurred in more than one third of all the president-cabinet relations analyzed in eight post-communist countries during the period 1991–2011. Some instances of these conflicts—for example, between President Yushchenko and Prime Minister Yanukovych in Ukraine in 2006–2007, and between President Băsescu and Prime Minister Ponta in Romania in 2012—resulted in political instability and impasse.

Table 3.7 reports on the level of intra-executive conflict as measured by Elgie (2018a) and Sedelius and Mashtaler (2013). Both of these studies use expert surveys to estimate the level of conflict between the president

Table 3.7 Intra-executive conflict and presidential power: Elgie (2018a) and Sedelius and Mashtaler (2013) scores

	Instances of conflict Elgie 1995–2015 No. of high-level conflict/No. of cabinet units	Instances of conflict Sedelius and Mashtaler 1991–2012 No. of high-level conflict/No. of cabinet units	Presidential power Doyle and Elgie	Presidential power Siaroff
Premier-presidentialism				
Ireland	0/8	–	0.062	2
Croatia 2001–	0/4	1/3	0.291	3
Finland	1/10	–	0.050	1
France	1/10	–	0.131	6
Bulgaria	2/7	4/8	0.183	2
Slovenia	2/13	–	0.118	0
Lithuania	3/15	4/12	0.282	3
Portugal	2/9	–	0.197	2
Moldova 1991–2000	–	1/4	0.241	4
Poland	4/13	7/14	0.241	2
Slovakia 1999–	3/8	–	0.189	1
Romania	7/15	3/9	0.250	4
Ukraine 2006–2010	–	2/3	0.329	–
President-parliamentarism				
Croatia 1991–2000	0/6	0/3	0.335	5
Austria	1/10	–	0.092	0
Russia	–	2/10	0.561	6
Iceland	7/15	–	0.325	0
Ukraine 1996–2005	–	5/9	0.464	7
Total	45/180	29/75		

Note: Countries arranged in order of frequencies of conflict as recorded by Elgie (2018a). Elgie (2018a) and Sedelius and Mashtaler (2013) use expert surveys to estimate the level of conflict between the president and the cabinet and they indicate high-level conflict as "the situation where there was persistent and severe conflict between the president and the cabinet" (Elgie 2018a: 130)
Source: Elgie (2018a), Sedelius and Mashtaler (2013)

and the cabinet and they indicate high-level conflict as "the situation where there was persistent and severe conflict between the president and the cabinet" (Elgie 2018a: 130). Obviously, the estimation of conflict varies between coders, which is also confirmed by an inter-coder reliability test by Elgie (2018a). Sedelius and Mashtaler use a combination of expert estimations and written sources where they recorded cases of high-level conflict only where they found confirmation by at least two independent documents or literature sources. Elgie's dataset covers a larger set of European countries (21, including Finland) and cabinet units (235) and has a later end-date (Dec 2014–Aug 2015) than Sedelius and Mashtaler's, who cover eight countries in Eastern Europe across 76 cabinet units over the post-communist period from mid-1990 to early 2012.

The estimations in Table 3.7 suggest that Sedelius and Mashtaler on average have used a lower threshold than Elgie for recording a cabinet-president unit as conflictive, but the overall pattern is quite similar. With the exception of Ireland, there are identified instances of intra-executive conflict by at least one of the two measures in all of the listed semi-presidential countries. These descriptive figures do indicate that conflict between the president and the cabinet is a quite frequently occurring phenomenon. There is furthermore a slight but apparent tendency that the countries with weaker presidential powers (columns 3 and 4) have fewer recorded cases of conflict. This is also statistically confirmed by Elgie (2018a: 139–143) when he applies a larger set of countries and more president-cabinet units. In a logistic regression test, he finds that presidential power is a stronger predictor of intra-executive conflict than other theoretically expected factors tested in the literature, including, for example, cohabitation, minority government, non-partisan presidents, and economic recession.

For our three cases, we see that there is notable variation on intra-executive conflict. Looking more closely into president-cabinet relations in our three countries, Table 3.8 reports on presidents, prime ministers, governing parties, cohabitation (yes/no), and intra-executive conflict (low/high).

Although subsequent chapters will reveal that manifest tensions have occurred between presidents and prime ministers in Finland from time to time, there is only one recorded instance of high-level conflict in Elgie's data. This concerned the cohabitation period between President Halonen and Prime Minister Vanhanen, where the two executives entered into open dispute about who would represent Finland in

Table 3.8   Intra-executive conflict and periods of cohabitation

President (party)	Prime minister	Prime minister's party	Cohabitation Y/N	Intra-ex conflict
Finland				
Mauno Koivisto (SDP)	Kalevi Sorsa (Feb	SDP	N	–
Jan 1982–Mar 1994	1982–Apr 1987)	KOK	N	–
	Harri Holkeri (Apr 1987–Apr 1991)	KESK	Y	–
	Esko Aho (Apr 1991–)			
Martti Ahtisaari (SDP)	Esko Aho (–Apr 1995)	KESK	Y	Low
Mar 1994–Mar 2000	Paavo Lipponen (Apr 1995–)	SDP	N	Low
Tarja Halonen (SDP)	Paavo Lipponen (–Apr	SDP	N	Low
Mar 2000–Mar 2012	2003)	KESK	Y	**High**
	Matti Vanhanen (Jun 2003–Jun 2010)	KESK	Y	Low
	Mari Kiviniemi (Jun 2010–Jun 2011)	KOK	N	Low
	Jyrki Katainen (Jun 2011–)			
Sauli Niinistö (KOK)	Jyrki Katainen (–Jun	KOK	N	Low
Mar 2012–	2014)	KOK	N	Low
	Alexander Stubb (Jun 2014–May 2015)	KESK	N	Low
	Juha Sipilä (May 2015–)			
Lithuania				
Algirdas M. Brazauskas	Adolfas Šleževičius	LDDP	N	Low
(LDDP)	(Mar 1993–Feb 1996)	LDDP	N	Low
Nov 1992–Feb 1998	Laurynas Stankevičius (Feb 1996–Dec 1996)	TS-LK	Y	Low
	Gediminas Vagnorius (Dec 1996–)			
Valdas Adamkus	Gediminas Vagnorius	TS-LK	N	**High**
(formally non-party)	(–May 1999)	TS-LK	N	–
Feb 1998–Feb 2003	Rolandas Paksas (Jun 1999–Oct 1999)	TS-LK	N	Low
	Andrius Kubilius (Nov 1999–Nov 2000)	TS-LK	N	**High**
	Rolandas Paksas (Nov 2000–Jun 2001)	LSDP	N	Low
	Algirdas M. Brazauskas (Jul 2001–)			

(*continued*)

Table 3.8 (continued)

President (party)	Prime minister	Prime minister's party	Cohabitation Y/N	Intra-ex conflict
Rolandas Paksas (LDP) Feb 2003–Apr 2004	Algirdas M. Brazauskas	LSDP	Y	High
Valdas Adamkus (formally non-party) Jul 2004–Jul 2009	Algirdas M. Brazauskas (–Jun 2006) Gediminas Kirkilas (Jul 2006–Dec 2008) Andrius Kubilius (Dec 2008–)	LSDP LSDP TS-LKD	N N N	High Low Low
Dalia Grybauskaitė (formally non-party) Jul 2009	Andrius Kubilius (– Dec 2012) Algirdas Butkevičius (Dec 2012–Dec 2016) Saulius Skvernelis (Dec 2016–)	TS-LKD LSDP LVZS	N N N	Low High Low
Romania				
Ion Iliescu (FSN, 1992, FSDN 1996, PDSR) Dec 1989–Nov 1996	Petre Roman (Dec 1989–Oct 1991) Theodor Stolojan (Oct 1991–Nov 1992) Nicolae Văcăroiu (Nov 1992–)	FSN PNL Non-party; 1993 PDSR	N N N	High Low Low
Emil Constantinescu (PNT-CD) Nov 1996–Dec 2000	Nicolae Văcăroiu (–Dec 1996) Victor Ciorbea (Dec 1996–Mar 1998) Radu Vasile (Apr 1998–Dec 1999) Constantin Isărescu (Dec 1999–Dec 2000)	PDSR PNT-CD PNT-CD Non-party	N N N N	Low Low High Low
Ion Iliescu (PDSR 2001; PSD, PD 2004) Dec 2000–Dec 2004	Adrian Nastase (Dec 2000–Dec 2004)	PDSR; 2001 PSD	N	Low
Traian Băsescu (PD) Dec 2004–Dec 2014	Calin Popescu-Tăriceanu (Dec 2004– Dec 2008) Emil Boc (Dec 2008–Feb 2012) Victor Ponta (May 2012–)	PNL PDL PSD	Y N Y	High Low High

(*continued*)

Table 3.8 (continued)

President (party)	Prime minister	Prime minister's party	Cohabitation Y/N	Intra-ex conflict
Klaus Iohannis (PNL) Dec 2014–	Victor Ponta (–Nov 2015)	PSD	Y	**High**
		Non-party	N	–
	Dacian Cioloş (Nov 2015–Jan 2017)	PSD	Y	–
	Sorin Grindeanu (Jan 2017–Jun 2017)	PSD	Y	–
	Mihai Tudose (Jun 2017–Jan 2018)			
	Vasilica Dăncilă (Jan 2018–)			

Note: Cohabitation is defined here "as the situation where the president and prime minister are from different parties and where the president's party is not represented in cabinet" (Elgie 2018b). For explanations on intra-executive conflict, see Table 3.7.
Party abbreviations. **Finland**: *KESK* Suomen Keskusta (Center of Finland), *KOK* Kansallinen Kokoomus (National Coalition, center-right), *SDP* Suomen Sosialidemokraattinen Piolue (Social Democratic Party of Finland). **Lithuania**: *LDP* Liberalų Demokratų Partija (Liberal Democratic Party), *LDDP* Lietuvos Demokratinė Darbo Partija (Democratic Labour Party of Lithuania), *LLS* Lietuvos Liberalų Sąjung (Liberal Union of Lithuania), *LSDP* Lietuvos Socialdemokratų Partija (Social Democratic Party of Lithuania), *LVZS* Lietuvos Valstiečių ir Žaliųjų Sąjunga (Lithuanian Peasant and Greens Union, agrarian, centrist, Green conservative), *TS-LK* Tėvynės Sąjunga-Lietuvos Konservatoriai (Homeland Union-Conservatives of Lithuania); *TS-LKD* Tėvynės Sąjunga-Lietuvos Krikščionys Demokratai (Homeland Union-Christian Democrats of Lithuania). **Romania**: *FSN* Frontul Salvării Naţionale (National Salvation Front, split from PCR, 22 Dec 1989–31 Mar 1993, then PD); *PD* Partidul Democrat (Democratic Party, Social Democratic, former FSN, 1993–2007, merged into PDL); *PDL* Partidul Democrat Liberal (Democratic Liberal Party, center-right, merger of PD and Partidul Liberal Democrat [Liberal Democratic Party], est. 2007); *PDSR* Partidul Democraţiei Sociale din România (Party of Social Democracy in Romania, ex-communist, former FSDN, 10 Jul 1993–16 Jan 2001, merged into PSDR); *PNL* Partidul Naţional Liberal (National Liberal Party, liberal, center-right, 1875–1938, 1944–1947, re-est. 1990); *PNT-CD* Partidul Naţional Ţărănesc Creştin Democrat (Christian Democratic National Peasants' Party, Christian democratic, PNT successor, est. 1990); *PSD* Partidul Social Democrat (Social Democrat Party, Social Democratic, merger of PDSR and PSDR, est. 16 Jan 2001); *PSDR* Partidul Social Democrat Român (Romanian Social Democratic Party, Social Democratic, 1910–1916, 1927–1938, 1944–Feb 1948, merged with PMR, restored 1990–16 Jan 2001, merged into PSD); *UNPR* Uniunea Naţională pentru Progresul României (National Union for the Progress of Romania, Social Democratic, split from PSD, est. Mar 2010)
Source: Data adapted from Elgie (2018a, b), Sedelius and Mashtaler (2013), World Statesmen (2018) www.worldstatesmen.org

the European Council in 2009. Before the Lisbon Treaty, the president had participated in the majority of the European Council meetings usually together with the foreign minister, but the Lisbon Treaty required one single representative. Ultimately, the conflict was resolved when the parliament adopted a bill for amending the constitution stating that the prime minister represents Finland in the European Council (the content and outcome of this dispute are further described in Chap. 6). But overall, executive relations in Finland are characterized by consensus seeking and by highly regulated relations between the president and the prime minster. Detailed regulations and a shared understanding among the political elites about keeping strict limits to presidential interference in policy-making have apparently limited presidential activism since the 2000 constitutional reform.

The semi-presidential system in Lithuania has come to be regarded as comparatively stable throughout the post-communist period. Power-sharing with low levels of conflict has characterized the president-prime minister relationship for the most part. Yet, all four presidents in Lithuania since independence have at some point entered into open conflict with the prime minister. We will describe each of these instances in more detail in Chaps. 5 and 6, but in general these conflicts are related to a stronger presidency than in Finland and to less detailed constitutional rules, which are open to competing jurisdictional interpretations by the president and the prime minister. The picture of relative institutional harmony in Lithuania is, however, somewhat blurred by the so-called Paksasgate, the short presidency of Rolandas Paksas which ended with his impeachment from office in 2003. Paksas' serious troubles started by accusations that the president and some of his senior staff had links with organized crime and Russian foreign intelligence service. A parliamentary commission was established and found that 'the President has been and is still vulnerable' and that Paksas had violated the constitution. This was sufficient for the Seimas to initiate impeachment proceedings. The Constitutional Court finally ruled that Paksas had indeed violated the constitution and his presidential oath. As a consequence, Paksas was formally voted out of office by the parliament.

Romania has experienced more instances of severe intra-executive conflict than both Finland and Lithuania (these conflicts are again described in more detail in Chaps. 5 and 6). Although the president's role in policy-making is constitutionally weak, the Romanian presidents have exercised considerable political influence, although to a different extent and for different reasons. Already from the outset of the transition period, there was intense conflict culminating in violent demonstrations between President Iliescu and Prime Minister Roman. Iliescu created the image and expectation that the president should be highly influential. There is, however, a marked difference between how Iliescu and his successors have perceived their roles as presidents. While the latter have largely refrained from intervening openly in the management of the cabinet, the former was involved in practically all aspects of policy-making, including in the direction of government coalitions.

President Iliescu interfered in both domestic and foreign affairs. The president's appointment of Nicolae Văcăroiu in 1992—a technical prime minister with a managerial role—ensured the continued involvement of the president in the direction of government policies. Prime Minister Vacariou was dependent on Iliescu's leverage over a diverse left-nationalist coalition, which supported the government (Verheijen 1999). President Constantinescu acted less dominantly and did not enjoy Iliescu's strong position within his own party and within the government coalition. But over time, and as the perception among Romanians grew that the center-right cabinet was unable to reform the economy effectively, Constantinescu became more directly involved in policy development. And during the latter period of his term, he chose to give up support for Prime Minister Vasile, with whom he had not been on good terms for quite some time (Vasile and Constantinescu both belonged to the political center-right organization, the Democratic Convention). After the prime minister became politically weakened, first by withdrawal of one of the coalition parties and later by the resignation of more than half of the ministers in the government, Constantinescu forced the prime minister to step down in December 1999—allegedly in conflict with the premier-presidential constitution. Expectedly, the opposition accused Constantinescu of not acting in accordance with the constitution. Article 85 of the constitution reads: "in the event of government modification or vacancy of office, the president shall dismiss and appoint, on the proposal of the prime minister, some members of the government". Vasile refused to resign, accusing Constantinescu of violating the constitution, and the matter was ultimately resolved after the prime minister resigned in exchange for his nomination as the chairman of the parliament's upper chamber (Blondel and Penescu 2001).

As revealed by the data in Table 3.8, the two latter presidents, Traian Băsescu and Klaus Iohannis, were involved in intra-executive conflict primarily during periods of cohabitation. In the literature, cohabitation, "where the president and prime minister are from opposing parties and where the president's party is not represented in cabinet" (Elgie 2011: 12), is portrayed both as a risk and as a built-in flexibility of semi-presidentialism (Sartori 1994). For example, France has experienced three instances of cohabitation and survived quite well by shifting power toward the prime minister and operate much as a parliamentary regime.[1] However, although established democracies have largely avoided severe consequences of cohabitation for political stability (Elgie and McMenamin 2011), scholars have warned that it is more challenging for transitional countries (Beuman 2016; Kirschke 2007; Suleiman 1994). In Romania, cohabitation has repeatedly generated clashes. The periods of cohabitation between President Băsescu and Prime Minister Popescu-Tăriceanu in 2007–2008 and between President Băsescu and Prime Minister Ponta in 2012–2014 were indeed marked by intense conflict and government crises, which even escalated into attempts of impeachment against President Băsescu (Gerghina and Miscoiu 2013). Similarly, cohabitation in 2017 between Băsescu's successor, the center-right President Klaus Iohannis, and Prime Minister Grindeanu from the Social Democratic Party (PSD) contained severe tensions propelled by anti-government protests, referendum threats, and even warnings of presidential suspension. In early 2017, hundreds of thousands of people took to the streets in Bucharest to protest government plans to decriminalize official misconduct and provide amnesty for some non-violent crimes. The government maintained that such pardon measures were necessary in order to adjust the Criminal Code with Constitutional Court rulings, reduce pressure on overcrowded prisons, and avoid sanctions from the European Court of Human Rights due to poor standards of prison conditions. President Iohannis publicly sided with the protesters against the cabinet and demanded that the government abandon the ordinance bill. The confrontation escalated when the president announced intentions to take the bill to referendum using his power to call a consultative referendum on matters of national interest (Bucur 2017). The government finally repealed the ordinance, but Grindeanu's cabinet had lost a great deal of support both among the population and within the Social Democratic Party. Ultimately, a parliamentary vote of no confidence in June 2017 ended the short-lived Grindeanu cabinet as well as the confrontational cohabitation between the president and the prime minister.

3.4   Public Trust in the President and Other Institutions

We now turn to the citizens and public support in semi-presidential regimes. Surveys in both parliamentary and semi-presidential countries suggest that citizens often express trust in their presidents, while they at the same time reveal more negative attitudes to other political leaders and institutions including the prime minister and the parliament. Tables 3.9 and 3.10 provide a general picture of trust in political and public institutions for the Baltic countries—for comparative reason we also include the

Table 3.9 Trust in institutions 2001–2014, Estonia, Latvia, Lithuania (percentages)

	Estonia				Latvia				Lithuania			
Year/change	2001	2004	2014	−/+	2001	2004	2014	−/+	2001	2004	2014	−/+
Courts	27	46	56	+29	23	35	29	+6	16	26	25	+9
Police	19	45	61	+42	27	36	31	+4	26	33	40	+14
Army	39	57	68	+29	35	36	38	+3	35	62	48	+13
Parties	8	7	11	+3	8	10	4	−4	8	10	7	−1
Parliament	11	18	18	+7	9	14	8	−1	9	17	8	−1
Government	–	–	19	–	–	–	10	–	–	–	15	–
President	59	69	41	−18	63	51	29	−34	57	63	33	−24
Prime minister	16	–	21	+5	36	–	17	−19	42	–	25	−17

Note: The survey item reads: "To what extent do you trust each of the following institutions to look after your interest?" 'Trust' is coded as those who rated the institution between 5 and 7 on a 7-point scale (1 = no trust at all, 7 = great trust)
Source: New Baltic Barometer (2001, 2004), Ekman et al. (2014)

Table 3.10 Trust in institutions 2001–2016, Czech Republic, Poland, Romania (percentages)

	Czech Republic				Poland				Romania			
Year/change	2001	2004	2016	−/+	2001	2004	2016	−/+	2001	2004	2016	−/+
Courts	34	26	27	−7	25	22	35	+10	19	26	37	+18
Police	40	28	38	−2	36	36	39	+3	24	33	42	+18
Army	39	29	45	+6	60	59	52	−8	62	60	67	+5
Parties	22	15	9	−13	9	3	11	+2	9	9	9	0
Parliament[a]	20	13	11	−9	20	9	17	−3	13	15	10	−3
Government	–	–	14	–	–	–	18	–	–	–	11	–
President	37	51	34	−3	65	40	28	−37	42	44	22	−20
Prime minister	27	–	16	−11	35	–	22	−13	42	–	17	−25

Note: The survey item reads: "To what extent do you trust each of the following institutions to look after your interest?" 'Trust' is coded as those who rated the institution between 5 and 7 on a 7-point scale (1 = no trust at all, 7 = great trust). [a]In the surveys up until 2001 the question asked about 'MPs' and from 2004 onward about 'Parliament'
Source: New Europe Barometer (2001, 2004), Ekman et al. (2016)

parliamentary countries Estonia and Latvia—2001, 2004, and 2014, and for three premier-presidential countries in Central Europe, the Czech Republic, Poland, and Romania—2001, 2004, and 2016. Three of these listed institutions—the court system, the police, and the army—represent 'repressive' state institutions and are (expected to be) less political and conflictual than the listed political institutions—parties, parliament, government, and president. We would in general expect trust in such state institutions to be more solid and stable than trust in institutions dominated by politicians. Parties, prime ministers, and parliament are more likely to be viewed by citizens as representatives of certain policy directions, electoral ambitions, and elite interests rather than as guardians of state and nation (Kitschelt 1995). The president is somewhere in between: political and personal, but largely elevated from day-to-day party politics. The survey item reported here reads '*to what extent do you trust the [government/parliament/president] to look after your interests?*' and is supposed to tap trust in certain institutions rather than in the incumbent/s who currently is in power. We should be aware, though, that in surveys of this kind citizens might not make strong distinctions between certain institutions and the individuals who fill them. In other words, perceptions of the incumbent/s most likely color the evaluation of the institution itself.

The reported surveys indeed confirm that trust in repressive state institutions is well above the levels of trust in political institutions and has increased since the beginning of the millennium, but considerably more in Estonia than in Latvia and Lithuania and more in Romania than in the Czech Republic and Poland. On the contrary and with the possible exception of Estonia, trust in political institutions has dropped or at best remained at similar levels over the period. Looking specifically at trust in the president, the figures are quite striking. Enjoying trust from a majority of citizens for a long time (see the New Europe Barometer 1–6)—also in the 1990s—the 2014 and 2016 data seem to represent a shift in public support for the presidency. With the caveat that these figures might be colored by the person currently holding office as well as certain domestic events, there is a larger than 15 percent drop in public support for the president across all the included countries (except for the Czech Republic), and in all cases the levels are well below 50 percent. It thus seems that the Central European presidents are gradually facing the trust levels of other political institutions such as parliament and government. However, also for these latter institutions, the trend looks anything but encouraging with levels below 20 percent in most cases. Thus, the long-term trust gap between the president and the prime minister largely remains in the 2014–2016 data.

Turning to Finland and public opinion on how the president is perceived in relation to the parliament, Figs. 3.1 and 3.2 show the trend from 1990 to 2017. In this survey the respondents were asked to evaluate whether they think a specific institution has 'too little' power, 'just enough/appropriate amount' of power, or 'too much' power. The trend largely follows the constitutional distribution of power over time. Back in

PRESIDENT'S POWER

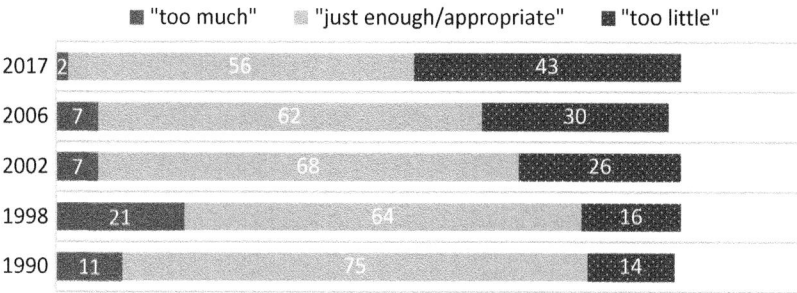

Fig. 3.1 Public evaluation of the powers of the president in Finland 1990–2017, percentages. (Source: Arvo- ja asennetutkimus/EVA Attitude and Value Survey 2017, www.eva.fi)

PARLIAMENT'S (EDUSKUNTA) POWER

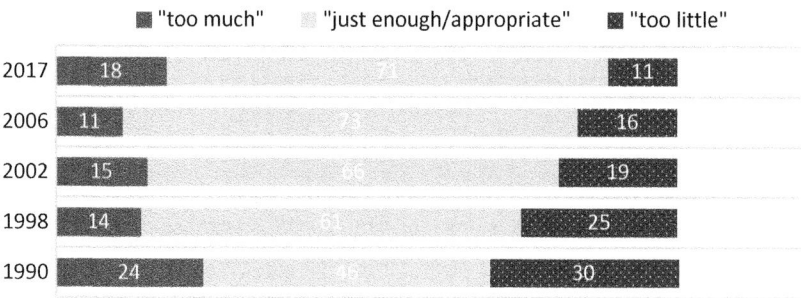

Fig. 3.2 Public evaluation of the powers of the parliament in Finland 1990–2017, percentages. (Source: Arvo- ja asennetutkimus/EVA Attitude and Value Survey 2017, www.eva.fi)

1990 when the president still possessed a considerably larger share of formal prerogatives and where the Cold War era was just about to end, 75 percent of the respondents expressed that the president's power was 'just enough/appropriate' (Fig. 3.1). Over the period, this share has gradually declined, whereas the group that thinks that the president has 'too little' power has increased considerably. Interestingly, a sharp rise in support of stronger presidential powers came in 2002—two years after the reformed constitution in which presidential powers were significantly curtailed. This trend has continued over the period following the president's weakening executive role in both domestic and EU affairs, and in 2017 the share of respondents who consider that the president has 'too little' power has risen to 43 percent. On a reversed but logical parallel, Fig. 3.2 reveals that the share of respondents who are satisfied with the amount of parliament's power has increased from 46 percent in 1990 to 71 percent in 2017.

Looking more closely into specific areas where public opinion supports that the president should have strong powers, Fig. 3.3 shows some inter-

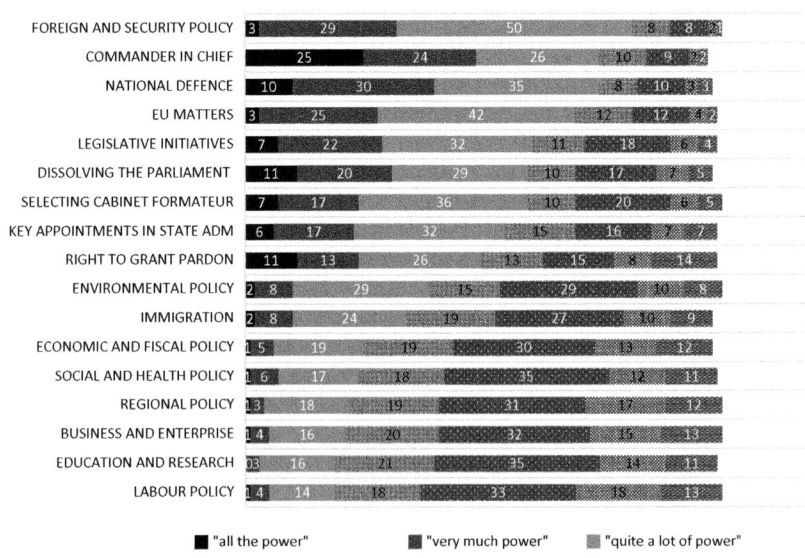

Fig. 3.3 Public opinion on presidential power in Finland 2018, percentages. (Source: Arvo- ja asennetutkimus/EVA Attitude and Value Survey 2018, www.eva.fi)

esting patterns. These public survey data from 2018 suggest that almost 70 percent or more agree that the president should have 'all the power', 'very much power', or 'quite a lot of powers' in areas of EU matters, national defense, and foreign and security policy. On foreign and security policy, this support is above 80 percent. Furthermore, about 60 percent express that the president should have 'very much power' or 'quite a lot of power' in dissolving the parliament and selecting the government formateur. As the items tap into more typically domestic policy areas, support for presidential powers decreases and the majority agree that the president should have 'quite little power', 'very little power', or 'no power at all' in, for example, social and health policy, economic policy, education and research, and labor market policy.

Overall, these data seem to support the idea of executive power-sharing in semi-presidential regimes. The president is expected to be a significant actor in matters of foreign and security affairs and more than just a ceremonial figure in government formation and legislative politics. In fact, our data suggest that citizens in Finland were more content with the stronger position of the president in the 1990s under the pre-2000 constitution than they are with the weaker president in the 2000s. However, while Finnish presidents are highly respected and popular among the citizens, there is a shared view among the political elites about a highly restricted role of the president. In particular, this applies to government formation where the legacy of Kekkonen's dominance over prime minister selections and cabinet minister nominations looms over the political system (described in more detail in Chap. 5). This apparent gap between a collective understanding among the political elites about a weak presidency on the one side and citizen support of a significantly stronger president on the other may be effectively exploited by the presidents from time to time.

As mentioned in Chap. 2, the greater popularity of presidents as compared with prime ministers, parties, and parliamentarians allows them to interpret their role as spokesmen for popular discontent and to publicly criticize the government (Krupavičius 2013; Raunio and Sedelius 2017). In the post-communist context, trust in the presidency can also be viewed in light of strong political characters in the early days of transition such as Vaclav Havel in Czechoslovakia/Czech Republic, Lech Walesa in Poland, and to some extent also Ion Iliescu[2] in Romania, who earned a reputation as political dissidents in the late communist era (Taras 1997: 16). The first generation of post-communist prime ministers, by contrast, were in most cases less well known within and outside their respective countries.

Prime ministers possess the bulk of formal powers within the executive but often fall short on legitimacy among citizens at large. The presidents, for their part, find that their popularity outweigh their formal powers and political influence. This in itself is enough to create an imbalance in claims of democratic legitimacy between the two actors. And it might be that the presidents' limited constitutional powers actually account for some of their greater popularity among the public. The basic point, however, is that this gap between perceived legitimacy and formal powers is significant for understanding institutional logics of semi-presidentialism as well as the frequent occurrences of intra-executive tensions between the president and the cabinet.

3.5   A COMPARATIVE DESIGN WITH EXPLORATIVE AMBITIONS

As revealed by this chapter, our three selected countries represent varying semi-presidential experiences that we believe serve quite neatly the subsequent analysis of executive coordination mechanisms. To just briefly summarize our argument: the selection is based on a most-similar logic (Przeworski and Teune 1970; Lijphart 1971) to the extent that we are dealing with three European premier-presidential democracies embedded in the EU. Finland's long-term experience of enduring democracy under semi-presidentialism is comparatively attractive when analyzing the newer experiences of semi-presidentialism in Lithuania and Romania. Finland aside, there is the shared legacy of systemic communism in Lithuania and Romania, their subsequent transition to democracy and market economy in the 1990s, and their EU and NATO accession processes in the 2000s. Following a most-similar logic we, furthermore, have notable variation on our key variables of interest, presidential activism, and intra-executive conflict. In an ideal most-similar system design, this variation should be attributed to apparent dissimilarities between cases that otherwise share basic fundaments. Thus, at the outset we would relate the marked difference on the level of presidential activism and conflict between Finland and Romania to apparent contextual differences such as level of corruption, democratic, and political stability, and to institutional dissimilarities of their semi-presidential systems including presidential powers, cohabitation, and party and electoral system dynamics. Arguably, Finland and Romania represent our most contrasting cases, whereas Lithuania represents a case in between, sharing with Romania many of the attributes followed by the post-communist transition, as well as a semi-presidential constitution that provides the presidency with quite significant powers. Interestingly, however, although Lithuania has experienced several instances of presidential activism, there are relatively few observations of severe intra-executive conflict over the course of the post-communist period. Thus, to account for this difference between Lithuania and Romania, we would trace dissimilarities in differing transitional and political trajectories and in varying institutional features of their semi-presidential systems. Adding to this puzzle, we introduce executive coordination mechanisms between the president and the prime minister as an intervening variable positioned between the key explanatory factors and the level of presidential activism (see Chap. 2).

However, small-n studies have a number of well-recognized limitations (George and Bennet 2005; King et al. 1994; Ragin 1987) and this study is no exception. There are at least three obvious and standard caveats to our study. First, there are many variables at play and any observed difference and similarity across the cases may well be caused by exogenous factors that are not fully accounted for by the research design. In other words, where we believe that explanatory factors such as institutional legacy, transitional context, presidential power, party and electoral system dynamics, and incumbents' personality matter to presidential activism and intra-executive conflict, there is certainly more to the equation than covered by our frame and data. Second, and although our design accounts for a number of relevant factors, these cannot be easily separated from one another and we are unlikely to disentangle sufficiently the causal chains of interaction. Hence, it is difficult to isolate the possible cause of one factor from another and we should be careful with causal interpretation of evidence based on this type of research design. Finally, and most obvious, we are dealing only with three European cases of semi-presidentialism over a limited period of time. Although we believe our cases to be strategically selected representations of differing semi-presidential paths and in this chapter also embedded in a wider comparative setting of semi-presidentialism, we cannot determine with certainty to what extent our findings carry valid lessons to the larger universe of semi-presidential regimes.

However, our design strategy does carry specific benefits to the cumulative knowledge of semi-presidentialism. On a comparative level, executive coordination mechanisms are something of a blind spot in the semi-presidential literature. Our small-n design with most-similar features and based on expert interviews and detailed documentation gives room for descriptive, explorative, and, to a certain extent, explanative avenues.

The focused comparison allows for uncovering systematically a set of operative mechanisms inside the semi-presidential system, of which little is revealed by previous literature. We therefore believe that our selected design contributes both theoretically and empirically on key institutional aspects of semi-presidentialism.

NOTES

1. A 2000 amendment of the French Constitution shortened the president's term of office from seven to five years and changed the electoral calendar so that presidential and legislative elections occur at the same time. This change has made it less likely that cohabitation will occur in the future.
2. In the post-communist period Iliescu somewhat benefited politically from the humiliations he suffered under Ceausescu after expressing disagreement with his way of ruling Romania in the 1980s.

BIBLIOGRAPHY

Åberg, J., & Denk, T. (2019, forthcoming). Diffusion as Explanation of Regime Choice at Democratization.

Anckar, C. (1999). Semipresidentialism: En taxonomisk betraktelse. *Historisk Tidskrift för Finland, 84*(4), 495–518.

Arter, D. (1999). Finland. In R. Elgie (Ed.), *Semi-Presidentialism in Europe* (pp. 48–66). Oxford: Oxford University Press.

Arvo- ja asennetutkimus/EVA Attitude and Value Survey. (2018). www.eva.fi/eng. Accessed 13 Dec 2018.

Bell, D. (2000). *Presidential Politics in the Fifth Republic.* London: Berg Publisher.

Bell, D., & Gaffney, J. (2013). *The Presidents of the French Fifth Republic.* London: Palgrave Macmillan.

Beuman, L. M. (2016). *Political Institutions in East Timor: Semi-Presidentialism and Democratisation.* Abingdon: Routledge.

Blondel, J., & Penescu, I. (2001). Romania. In J. Blondel & F. Müller-Rommel (Eds.), *Cabinets in Eastern Europe* (pp. 109–119). London: Palgrave Macmillan.

Bucur, C. (2017, March 15). Romania: President Postpones Anti-Corruption Referendum. *Presidential Power* blog. https://presidential-power.com/?p=6165

Doyle, D., & Elgie, R. (2016). Maximizing the Reliability of Cross-National Measures of Presidential Power. *British Journal of Political Science, 46*(4), 731–741.

Ekman, J., Duvold, K., & Berglund, S. (2014). *Baltic Barometer 2014* [Datafile]. Huddinge: Södertörn University.

Ekman, J., Duvold, K., & Berglund, S. (2016). *Social-Political Survey in Central Europe* [Datafile]. Huddinge: Södertörn University.

Elgie, R. (Ed.). (1999). *Semi-Presidentialism in Europe*. Oxford: Oxford University Press.

Elgie, R. (2010). Duverger, Semi-Presidentialism and the Supposed French Archetype. In E. Grossman & N. Sauger (Eds.), *France's Political Institutions at 50* (pp. 6–25). London: Routledge.

Elgie, R. (2011). *Semi-Presidentialism: Sub-Types and Democratic Performance*. Oxford: Oxford University Press.

Elgie, R. (2015). Presidential Power Scores. Dataset available at *Presidential Power*. https://presidential-power.com. Accessed 3 Oct 2018.

Elgie, R. (2018a). *Political Leadership: A Pragmatic Institutionalist Approach*. London: Palgrave Macmillan.

Elgie, R. (2018b). List of Cohabitations. *The Semi-Presidential One*. Blog post by Robert Elgie. www.semipresidentialism.com. Accessed 7 Oct 2018.

Elgie, R., & McMenamin, I. (2011). Explaining the Onset of Cohabitation under Semi-Presidentialism. *Political Studies, 59*(3), 616–635.

Elgie, R., & Moestrup, S. (Eds.). (2008). *Semi-Presidentialism in Central and Eastern Europe*. Manchester: Manchester University Press.

Freedom in the World 2018. (2018). www.freedomhouse.org. Accessed 4 Oct 2018.

George, A. L., & Bennet, A. (2005). *Case Studies and Theory Development in the Social Sciences*. Cambridge, MA: MIT Press.

Gerghina, S., & Miscoiu, S. (2013). The Failure of Cohabitation: Explaining the 2007 and 2012 Institutional Crises in Romania. *East European Politics and Societies and Cultures, 27*(4), 668–684.

Holm-Hansen, J. (2006). Litauen: sovjetrepublikken som fekk vesteuropeisk partimønster. In E. Bakke (Ed.), *Sentral-Europa og Baltikum etter 1989*. Oslo: Det Norske Samlaget.

Jung, J. K., & Deering, C. J. (2015). Constitutional Choices: Uncertainty and Institutional Design in Democratizing Nations. *International Political Science Review, 36*(1), 60–77.

King, G., Keohane, R. O., & Verba, S. (1994). *Designing Social Inquiry: Scientific Inference in Qualitative Research*. Princeton: Princeton University Press.

Kirschke, L. (2007). Semipresidentialism and the Perils of Power-Sharing in Neopatrimonial States. *Comparative Political Studies, 40*(11), 1372–1394.

Kitschelt, H. (1995). Formation of Party Cleavages in Post-Communist Democracies: Theoretical Propositions. *Party Politics, 1*(4), 447–472.

Krupavičius, A. (2013). Lithuania's President: A Formal and Informal Power. In V. Hloušek et al. (Eds.), *Presidents Above Parties? Presidents in Central and Eastern Europe. Their Formal Competencies and Informal Power* (pp. 205–232). Brno: Masaryk University.

Lazardeux, S. G. (2015). *Cohabitation and Conflicting Politics in French Policymaking*. Basingstoke: Palgrave Macmillan.

Lijphart, A. (1971). Comparative Politics and the Comparative Method. *American Political Science Review, 65*(3), 682–693.

Lijphart, A., & Waisman, C. H. (Eds.). (2006). *Institutional Design in New Democracies: Eastern Europe and Latin America.* Boulder: Westview Press.

List of Electoral Systems by Country. (2018). *Wikipedia.* https://en.wikipedia.org/wiki/List_of_electoral_systems_by_country. Accessed 2 Nov 2018.

Nations in Transit 2018. (2018). www.freedomhouse.org. Accessed 3 Oct 2018.

New Baltic Barometer 1-6, CSPP School of Government & Public Policy at the University of Strathclyde. www.cspp.strath.ac.uk. Accessed 2 Nov 2018.

New Europe Barometer 2001. "NDB VI Autumn. Dataset SPP 364.", CSPP School of Government & Public Policy at the University of Strathclyde. www.cspp.strath.ac.uk/nebo.html. Accessed 15 Sept 2016.

New Europe Barometer 2004. "NDB VII Winter. Dataset SPP 404.", CSPP School of Government & Public Policy at the University of Strathclyde. www.cspp.strath.ac.uk/nebo.html. Accessed 15 Sept 2016.

Nørgaard, O., & Johannsen, L. (Eds.). (1999). *The Baltic States After Independence.* Cheltenham: Edward Elgar.

Paloheimo, H. (2001). Divided Government in Finland: From a Semi-Presidential to a Parliamentary Democracy. In R. Elgie (Ed.), *Divided Government in Comparative Perspective* (pp. 86–105). Oxford: Oxford University Press.

Protsyk, O. (2005). Politics of Intra-Executive Conflict in Semi-Presidential Regimes in Eastern Europe. *East European Politics & Societies, 19*(2), 135–160.

Protsyk, O. (2006). Intra-Executive Competition Between President and Prime Minister: Patterns of Institutional Conflict and Cooperation under Semi-Presidentialism. *Political Studies, 54*(2), 219–244.

Przeworski, A., & Teune, H. (1970). *The Logic of Comparative Social Inquiry.* New York: Wiley.

Ragin, C. (1987). *The Comparative Method: Moving Beyond Qualitative and Quantitative Strategies.* Oakland: University of California Press.

Raunio, T., & Sedelius, T. (2017). Shifting Power-Centres of Semi-Presidentialism: Exploring Executive Coordination in Lithuania. *Government and Opposition,* First view. https://doi.org/10.1017/gov.2017.31

Sartori, G. (1994). *Comparative Constitutional Engineering: An Inquiry into Structures, Incentives and Outcomes.* Basingstoke: Macmillan.

Sedelius, T. (2006). *The Tug-of-War between Presidents and Prime Ministers: Semi-Presidentialism in Central and Eastern Europe.* Örebro: Örebro Studies in Political Science 15.

Sedelius, T. (2008). Demokrati eller presidentdiktatur: Konstitutionella vägval i postkommunistiska länder. *Nordisk Østforum, 22*(2), 141–161.

Sedelius, T., & Ekman, J. (2010). Intra-executive Conflict and Cabinet Instability: Effects of Semi-Presidentialism in Central and Eastern Europe. *Government and Opposition, 45*(4), 505–530.

Sedelius, T., & Mashtaler, O. (2013). Two Decades of Semi-Presidentialism: Issues of Intra-executive Conflict in Central and Eastern Europe 1991–2011. *East European Politics, 29*(2), 109–134.

Shugart, M. S., & Carey, J. M. (1992). *Presidents and Assemblies: Constitutional Design and Electoral Dynamics.* New York: Cambridge University Press.

Siaroff, A. (2003). Comparative Presidencies: The Inadequacy of the Presidential, Semi-Presidential and Parliamentary Distinction. *European Journal of Political Research, 42*(3), 287–312.

Suleiman, E. N. (1994). Presidentialism and Political Stability in France. In J. J. Linz & A. Valenzuela (Eds.), *The Failure of Presidential Democracy: Comparative Perspectives, Volume 1* (pp. 137–162). Baltimore: Johns Hopkins University Press.

Taras, R. (1997). Separating Power: Keeping Presidents in Check. In R. Taras (Ed.), *Postcommunist Presidents* (pp. 15–37). Cambridge: Cambridge University Press.

Transparency International. (2019). The Corruption Perception Index 2017. www.transparency.org. Accessed 2 Jan 2019.

Verheijen, T. (1999). Romania. In R. Elgie (Ed.), *Semi-Presidentialism in Europe* (pp. 193–2015). Oxford: Oxford University Press.

World Statesmen. (2018). www.worldstatesmen.org. Accessed 2 Oct 2018.

CHAPTER 4

Formal Coordination Mechanisms

In our theoretical framework in Chap. 2 we identified four different types of formal coordination mechanisms: bilateral meetings between the president and the prime minister; ministerial committees or joint councils between the president and the government; national security, foreign policy, or EU affairs councils; and coordination between civil servants of the offices of the prime minister and the president. In Chap. 2 we also discussed the different categories of institutions and the difficulties involved in drawing a clear line between formal and informal institutions. Here these difficulties apply particularly to bilateral exchanges between the president and the prime minister and to administrative coordination, as ministerial committees and various foreign policy councils are likely to derive their status from the constitution or other laws.

Regarding bilateral meetings, it is unlikely that they would be regulated by laws or decrees, and hence they should primarily be seen as informal institutions. Referring to the typology introduced in Chap. 2, bilateral meetings should be first and foremost regarded as complementary informal institutions, as their main purpose is to facilitate coordination between the two executives. However, insofar as they continue to exist independent of the individual office-holders, bilateral meetings can also be classified as de facto formal coordination mechanisms, and hence we include them in this chapter. Nonetheless, the informal nature of bilateral exchanges makes them also vulnerable to breaking down after the election of new office-holders. Turning to coordination between the offices of the

© The Author(s) 2020   79
T. Raunio, T. Sedelius, *Semi-Presidential Policy-Making in Europe*,
Palgrave Studies in Presidential Politics,
https://doi.org/10.1007/978-3-030-16431-7_4

president and the prime minister, again we find it unlikely that it would be subject to any formal rules. Instead, we interpret it as a complementary informal institution that is also designed to foster smoother dialogue and decision-making between the two executives. Administrative coordination is thus also a de facto formal instrument when such communication is regular and not dependent on individual office-holders.

4.1   ESTABLISHING VARIATION BETWEEN FINLAND, LITHUANIA, AND ROMANIA

Drawing on both legal provisions (constitutions, laws, decrees) and the in-depth interviews, Table 4.1 reports intra-executive coordination mechanisms in Finland, Lithuania, and Romania. For each instrument, the table specifies whether the mechanism is regulated by laws and also any changes over time or additional relevant remarks. Particularly the last column is important, as the table essentially summarizes for each country developments since the 1990s. It becomes immediately evident that there are significant differences between our three cases, with Finland having considerably more institutionalized coordination between the two executives than Lithuania and Romania. This applies particularly to regular bilateral exchanges and to ministerial committees. In line with our main theoretical argument, we should thus expect higher levels of presidential activism in Lithuania and Romania (Chaps. 5 and 6).

Bilateral Exchanges

In our theoretical framework, we assigned particular weight to bilateral, confidential exchanges between the two leaders. In Finland the system has remained the same ever since the new constitution entered into force in 2000. The president meets the prime minister essentially on a weekly basis, on Fridays before the plenary of the government and a potential meeting of the Ministerial Committee on Foreign and Security Policy. These bilateral meetings are very short, lasting normally at most half an hour, with normally no other persons present in the room. Interviews clearly confirm the importance of these bilateral exchanges, particularly in terms of identifying and solving potential intra-executive disagreements. While not based in any law or decree, the meetings have become an established practice not dependent on individual office-holders. No prime minister or president has questioned their importance and legitimacy, and

Table 4.1 Intra-executive coordination mechanisms in Finland, Lithuania, and Romania

	Yes/no			Legal status			Change over time/remarks		
	Fin	Lit	Rom	Fin	Lit	Rom	Fin	Lit	Rom
Bilateral meetings, president-prime minister	Yes	Yes	Yes, in relation to sensitive issues	No	No	No	Stable	Usually regular, dependent on office-holders	Dependent on office-holders
Joint councils or similar, president-government	No	No	No	No	No	No		Some existed during the presidencies of Brazauskas and Adamkus	
Ministerial committees where president is represented	Yes	No	No	Yes	No	No	Stable		
National security councils or equivalent where president and government are represented	No	Yes	Yes	No	Yes, defined by constitution and law	Yes, defined by constitution and law	The ministerial committee on foreign and security policy can be considered to perform this role		
Administrative coordination between the offices of the president and the prime minister	Yes	Yes	Yes	No	No	No			

it is very likely that such action by either executive would be strongly criticized by the political and administrative elites and the media.

Also the president and the foreign minister meet at least in principle on a weekly basis, normally before the prime minister meets the president. This is of course logical, as according to Section 93 of the constitution, "The communication of important foreign policy positions to foreign States and international organisations is the responsibility of the Minister with competence in foreign affairs". The meetings typically can last up to an hour. Civil servants from the Ministry for Foreign Affairs and the president's office can be present, but often the president and the foreign minister also continue discussions in private. As is the case with the bilateral exchanges between the president and the prime minister, the agenda of the meetings consists largely of more pressing foreign policy matters, including forthcoming meetings with foreign leaders. Good examples from recent years would be the situation in Russia and the neighboring Baltic region, relations with NATO, or the wars in Syria and the Middle East. EU issues are normally not discussed, with the exception of Common Foreign and Security Policy and Common Security and Defence Policy (CFSP/CSDP) matters. The president's office does, however, receive the agendas of the Foreign Affairs of the Council of the EU in advance.

In Lithuania and Romania, on the other hand, much depends on the party-political context and the presidents who have the initiative regarding such meetings. In Lithuania the presidents have by and large met prime ministers regularly, but presidents have also opted not to have such bilateral talks. For example, President Grybauskaitė has met the prime minister almost weekly, but for six months in 2016 there were no regular meetings with the premier. Also during the presidencies of Brazauskas and Adamkus, the regularity of meetings varied. According to Article 84(1) of the Lithuanian constitution, the president "shall decide the basic issues of foreign policy and, together with the Government, conduct foreign policy". It is only logical that cooperation between the president and the foreign minister is regular, although the exact frequency and forms of cooperation have varied between individual presidents.

In Romania there is no such institutionalized practice of bilateral exchanges between the prime minister and the president: instead, there are meetings or phone calls on various topics when the need arises. Overall, out of our three countries, the importance of party politics and especially cohabitation is definitely strongest in Romania, and this is also displayed in bilateral exchanges. Such interaction is certainly smoother and more active when the president and the prime minister share the same political affiliation (e.g. between Nicolae Văcăroiu and Ion Iliescu, Victor Ciorbea and Emil Constantinescu, and Emil Boc and Traian Băsescu). In such circumstances bilateral talks can take place weekly or even more often, and should be understood in the overall context of the president being actively involved in the work of his party. When the president and the prime minister come from opposing ideological camps, cooperation is less regular and has been in several instances clearly hampered by tensions between the two leaders. For example, in spring 2018 cooperation between President Iohannis and Prime Minister Dăncilă was difficult, with Iohannis accusing the prime minister of avoiding contacts (see Chap. 5). Also in Romania cooperation between the president and the foreign minister is less dependent on individual office-holders. The president is the highest representative of Romania abroad, but as in Finland and Lithuania, it is the foreign minister who represents the country in the EU's Foreign Affairs Council and also is responsible for much of the daily foreign affairs matters, and hence this alone creates strong incentives for coordination. Both the president and the foreign minister meet foreign leaders, and hence there is a need to ensure that the country is speaking with one voice.

Meetings with the Government

Finland is the only country utilizing ministerial committees, with the law on government recognizing four such committees: Ministerial Committee on Foreign and Security Policy, Ministerial Finance Committee, Ministerial Committee on Economic Policy, and, since 1995, Ministerial Committee on European Union Affairs. All four committees are chaired by the prime minister and bring together a subset of ministers, with all cabinet parties represented in each of the committees. These ministerial committees perform an important role in government decision-making, as the weekly government plenaries that bring together all ministers basically just rubber-stamp or give the formal approval to decisions taken in the ministerial committees or at the level of individual ministries. While the decree on government stipulates that the prime minister shall chair its meetings, ever since the new constitution entered into force, the sessions of the Ministerial Committee on Foreign and Security Policy have been chaired by the president. This was a consensual decision reached between the Social Democratic President Tarja Halonen and the Social Democratic Prime Minister Paavo Lipponen, and subsequent office-holders have respected the arrangement. In fact, officially the president is not even a member of the ministerial committee, and hence its sessions are called "joint meetings between the Ministerial Committee on Foreign and Security Policy and the President of the Republic" (TP-UTVA is the acronym in Finnish).[1] Perhaps to underline foreign policy co-leadership between the president and the government, the Ministerial Committee on Foreign and Security Policy does not convene without the president even though this would be perfectly possible.

Meeting regularly, roughly once a month, it performs an important function in the co-leadership of foreign and security policy between the president and the cabinet. The Finnish ministerial committee can also in a sense be perceived as a national security council, although without the presence of representatives of armed forces. The agenda consists of various foreign and security policy items, from crisis management operations to relations with Russia and other countries to participation in meetings of the United Nations and other international organizations, with national defense matters also on the agenda.[2] The Ministry for Foreign Affairs is responsible for preparing the meetings, hearing both the president and the prime minister in the process, and they last typically between one and one-and-a-half hour. The meetings usually take place after the bilateral meetings between the president and the prime minister, meaning thus that any serious disagreements between the two leaders can be discussed prior to the sessions of the ministerial committee. There are also presidential plenary sessions of the government chaired by the president, with all cabinet ministers present. The agenda of these sessions covers those issues still in the competence of the head of state. In these sessions, held roughly every two weeks, there is no voting and the president's decisions do not have to follow the opinion of the government.

All ministerial committees work behind closed doors, and a particular cloud of secrecy and confidentiality applies to the Ministerial Committee on Foreign and Security Policy. Interviewed politicians and civil servants were reluctant to reveal anything of its proceedings, and hence it is difficult to draw exact conclusions about the nature of the debates. Yet there is certainly more than anecdotal evidence suggesting that President Niinistö (2012–), who in any case chairs the meetings, has dominated the discussions. Niinistö has shared power with center-right prime ministers, and also particularly during the premiership of Juha Sipilä (2015–), the prime minister has clearly been content to leave the direction of foreign and security policy to the president. During the presidency of Halonen (2000–2012), the role of the president was more constrained. Social Democrat Halonen shared power from 2003 onward with center-right prime ministers, and overall her presidency was characterized by more tensions with the government. However, overall the tone in the ministerial committee is constructive and very much geared toward consensual decisions.

Security and Defence Policy Councils

None of the three countries employ more permanent joint councils that would bring together the president and members of the government. As will be discussed in Chap. 5, in Lithuania Presidents Brazauskas and Adamkus made use of some more short-term councils, and obviously presidents from all three countries have at different times set up various working groups or brought together relevant stakeholders to discuss a range of topics. In the realm of security and defense policy, the situation is very different. As discussed earlier, in Finland the Ministerial Committee on Foreign and Security Policy can be considered to perform a coordinating role in security policy, as the committee deals with all issues related to Finland's foreign and security policy, defense matters included. In Lithuania the functions and competence of the State Defence Council are defined in the constitution and in the Special Law on State Defence Council. According to Article 140 of the constitution:

> The main issues of State defence shall be considered and coordinated by the State Defence Council which consists of the President of the Republic, the Prime minister, the Speaker of the Seimas, the Minister of National Defence, and the Commander of the Armed Forces. The State Defence Council shall be headed by the President of the Republic. The procedure for its formation, activities, and its powers shall be established by law. The President of the Republic shall be the Commander-in-Chief of the Armed Forces of the State.

The State Defence Council is thus the highest coordinating body in matters related to Lithuanian security and defense policy. Matters on its agenda have focused on relations with Russia and developments in the neighboring areas, the North Atlantic Treaty Organization (NATO) membership, the organization of defense forces, including the reintroduction of conscription (see Chap. 6). The president chairs the meetings, and the work of the State Defence Council is very much in his hands. This applies particularly to the frequency of the Council's meetings: apart from external developments, notably the war in Ukraine from 2014 onward, influencing its schedule, it is up to the president to decide when the Council convenes.

Romania also has a similar special coordinating authority in security policy, the Supreme Council of National Defence (CSAT). The Council has its origins in the inter-war period, having first been established in the mid-1920s. It was then re-established in 1990 following democratization, with the current law defining its organization.[3] According to Article 119 of the constitution, "The supreme Council of National Defence shall unitarily organize and co-ordinate the activities concerning the country's defence and security, its participation in international security keeping, and in collective defence in military alliance systems, as well as in peace keeping or restoring missions". Chaired by the president, other members of the council are the prime minister, the minister of national defence, the minister of administration and interior, the minister of foreign affairs, the minister of justice, the minister of industry and resources, the minister of public finances, the director of the Romanian intelligence, the director of the foreign intelligence service, the chief of General Staff, and the presidential counselor on national security. The CSAT secretariat is located in the president's office. The Supreme Council of National Defence is convened on the initiative of the president (officially also one-third of CSAT members can demand that a meeting be organized), and essentially it meets when necessary, although normally around three times a year. As its composition indicates, the agenda of CSAT is quite broad and covers all types of security and defense policy issues, internal security included. The decisions of the Council are adopted by consensus and CSAT must report annually or when so required to the parliament (Apostolache 2016).

Furthermore, in Romania the president can chair those sessions of the full government where national security issues are on the agenda. According to Article 87 of the constitution, "the President of Romania may participate in the meetings of the Government debating upon matters of national interest with regard to foreign policy, the defence of the country, ensurance of public order, and, at the Prime minister's request, in other instances as well". Notably, the president needs to be invited to such meetings, and hence the frequency of the presidential sessions of the government depends not only on external developments but also on relations between the prime minister and the president. President Emil Constantinescu only used the prerogative three times, Ion Iliescu in his second term of office (2000–2004) seven times, whereas from 2004 to 2008, Traian Băsescu presided over ten governmental meetings (Dima 2009). During the four years of the presidency of Klaus Iohannis, such a presidential session has been convened only once. When the president attends the government meetings, he also chairs the proceedings. It is important to note that in all three countries it is the president who chairs the security councils. This clearly strengthens the position of the president both regarding when meetings are held and regarding actual decision-making in the sessions.[4]

Finally, turning to administrative coordination between the offices of the president and the prime minister, there is less variation between Finland, Lithuania, and Romania; although it appears that the system is least developed in Romania. This is of course logical when considering that in all three countries the two executives essentially need to exchange information in order to facilitate decision-making in matters where both the president and the prime minister are involved, such as appointments. Given that in all three cases the president either leads foreign and security policy or at least codirects it with the government, it is not surprising that such administrative coordination is most developed in external relations. The respective offices of the prime minister and the president exchange documents and information essentially on a daily basis, with the civil servants also meeting regularly, either bilaterally or in various bodies where both the president's office and the prime minister's office are represented. Presidential offices are also in very active contact with the foreign ministry, as in all three countries the foreign ministry is mainly responsible for handling day-to-day administration regarding foreign policy: communication with other countries and international organizations, preparing national positions, particularly those to be presented in the Foreign Affairs Council of the EU, and planning state visits abroad.

4.2   Explaining the Variation

Let us conclude this chapter by reflecting on the observed variation and the causal mechanisms behind the adopted intra-executive coordination models. As discussed in Chap. 2, institutional theory underlines the importance of initial decisions over policy or organizations that 'lock in' subsequent choices. It also emphasizes the role of critical junctures that can bring about fundamental change, rendering past practices illegitimate and ineffective. In all three countries the 1990s were such a critical juncture, but in different ways that also resulted in different outcomes.

In Finland the constitutional reform that weakened substantially the powers of the president was a deliberate and orderly process that enjoyed broad consensus among the political elites, both on the right and on the left. The various amendments to the constitution were introduced from the late 1980s onward, with the new constitution entering into effect in 2000. Given that the constitutional reform was strongly motivated by the long reign of President Kekkonen (1956–1981), during which power was very much centralized in the president, the deliberations in the constitutional reform process gave considerable attention to the question of how to 'reign in' or constrain the president. The directly elected presidency was to be maintained, but the president's constitutional prerogatives were to be strictly limited to foreign and security policy—and even where the president still had decision-making authority, the constitution and secondary legislation established rules that effectively bind the president to cooperation with the government. More specifically, the constitutional reform was partly necessitated by the impending EU membership (see Chap. 6). Without the reform, the president would have represented Finland in the European Council, and hence the question of ensuring parliamentary accountability of national EU policy was high on the agenda (Arter 1999; Jyränki 2000; Saraviita 2000; Nousiainen 2001; Husa 2011; Carrier 2016: 73–79; Karvonen et al. 2016).

In Lithuania and Romania the context was very different. Following the collapse of the Soviet bloc and the transition to democracy, in both countries—and in the Central and East European (CEE) region as a whole—the young democracies had more pressing concerns than the exact wordings of the constitution about presidential powers. Lithuania and Romania needed to take serious decisions about how their countries were to be governed, but it is perhaps understandable that in those circumstances the prerogatives of the presidency and particularly how to manage intra-executive relations were overshadowed by more important issues such as kick-starting the economy, foreign and defense policy, and in general just ensuring a smooth transition to democratic rule and market economy. In both countries there were also disagreements about the role of the president vis-à-vis the other state institutions.

In Lithuania such disagreements were also influenced by the public mood, linked to the popularity of the pro-independence movement *Sajūdis* leader Vytautas Landsbergis, which appeared to favor a strong leader. This was also shown by the May 1992 referendum 'on the restoration of the institution of the president', which aimed at the immediate establishment of the presidency. Around 69 percent voted in favor of the proposition, but the referendum failed to achieve the necessary threshold of 'yes' votes due to the low turnout (Urbanavičius 1999; Matsuzato and

Gudžinskas 2006; Krupavičius 2008, 2013; Norkus 2013; Urdze 2016). The role of the president was at the center of the discussions, and there were initial plans to issue a decree about coordination between the president and the other state institutions, but this idea was rejected.[5] The reasons for rejection included time pressure and political opposition, and also it was not perceived appropriate to regulate such matters by laws. However, it was nonetheless recognized that cooperation between the central state institutions was a prerequisite for successful policy-making (Brazauskas 2007: 63).

In Romania the initial transition to democracy was very much dominated by the National Salvation Front (NSF) and its leader Ion Iliescu, which won a landslide victory in the 1990 parliamentary elections. Iliescu also won the first presidential elections, held concurrently with the parliamentary elections, with 85 percent of the votes. Overall, the role of the presidency and its relations with the legislature and the government featured strongly in the discussions. Apart from introducing checks and balances to the political regime, the choice of a semi-presidential regime needs to be also understood in the context of Iliescu's popularity. The opposition was fragmented and hardly involved in drafting the constitution, with some opposition politicians arguing for a return to monarchy while other voices, also from inside the ruling NSF, called for a weaker, indirectly elected presidency. However, the establishment of direct elections for the president was not seriously questioned, even though there were also concerns about this leading to an unhealthy concentration of powers in the presidency (Verheijen 1999; Gallagher and Andrievici 2008; Guțan 2012; Perju 2015; Gherghina and Hein 2016; Elgie 2018: 215–249).

Notes

1. https://valtioneuvosto.fi/en/government/ministerial-committees; Laki valtioneuvostosta 28.2.2003/175, 24 §, https://www.finlex.fi/fi/laki/ajantasa/2003/20030175#L2P12
2. Valtioneuvoston ohjesääntö 3.4.2003/262, 25 §, https://www.finlex.fi/fi/laki/ajantasa/2003/20030262#L4P25
3. Law no. 415/2002[14] on the organization and functioning of the Supreme Council of National Defence, Official Gazette of Romania, Part I, issue 494/10.07.2002.
4. In addition, Article 86 of the Constitution stipulates that "The President of Romania may consult with the Government about urgent, extremely important matters".

5. Earlier version of the government's rules of the procedure (until 2009) had separate provisions about relations with the president, but these were of a rather general nature, stating, for example, that, on the initiative of the president, the government and the president could establish joint working groups or examine and take decisions on matters related to state administration.

BIBLIOGRAPHY

Apostolache, M. C. (2016). The Prime Minister and the Supreme Council of National Defence. *Journal of Law and Administrative Sciences, 6*(2016), 45–57.

Arter, D. (1999). Finland. In R. Elgie (Ed.), *Semi-Presidentialism in Europe* (pp. 48–66). Oxford: Oxford University Press.

Brazauskas, A. (2007). *Ir Tuomet Dirbome Lietuvai: Faktai, Atsiminimai, Komentarai.* Vilnius: Knygai.

Carrier, M. (2016). *Executive Politics in Semi-Presidential Regimes: Power Distribution and Conflicts Between Presidents and Prime Ministers.* Lanham: Lexington Books.

Dima, B. (2009). Semiprezidenţialismul românesc postdecembrist. *Sfera Politicii, 17*(139): 14–29. http://www.sferapoliticii.ro/sfera/139/art02-dimab.html

Elgie, R. (2018). *Political Leadership: A Pragmatic Institutionalist Approach.* London: Palgrave Macmillan.

Gallagher, T., & Andrievici, V. (2008). Romania: Political Irresponsibility Without Constitutional Safeguards. In R. Elgie & S. Moestrup (Eds.), *Semi-Presidentialism in Central and Eastern Europe* (pp. 138–158). Manchester: Manchester University Press.

Gherghina, S., & Hein, M. (2016). Romania. In A. Fruhstorfer & M. Hein (Eds.), *Constitutional Politics in Central and Eastern Europe: From Post-Socialist Transition to the Reform of Political Systems* (pp. 173–197). Wiesbaden: Springer.

Guţan, M. (2012). Romanian Semi-Presidentialism in Historical Context. *Romanian Journal of Comparative Law, 2,* 275–303.

Husa, J. (2011). *The Constitution of Finland: A Contextual Analysis.* Oxford: Hart Publishing.

Jyränki, A. (2000). *Uusi perustuslakimme.* Turku: Iura Nova.

Karvonen, L., Paloheimo, H., & Raunio, T. (Eds.). (2016). *The Changing Balance of Political Power in Finland.* Stockholm: Santérus Academic Press.

Krupavičius, A. (2008). Semi-Presidentialism in Lithuania: Origins, Development and Challenges. In R. Elgie & S. Moestrup (Eds.), *Semi-Presidentialism in Central and Eastern Europe* (pp. 65–84). Manchester: Manchester University Press.

Krupavičius, A. (2013). Lithuania's President: A Formal and Informal Power. In V. Hloušek et al. (Eds.), *Presidents Above Parties? Presidents in Central and*

Eastern Europe, Their Formal Competencies and Informal Power (pp. 205–232). Brno: Masaryk University.

Matsuzato, K., & Gudžinskas, L. (2006). An Eternally Unfinished Parliamentary Regime? Semipresidentialism as a Prism to View Lithuanian Politics. *Acta Slavica Iaponica, 23*, 146–170.

Norkus, Z. (2013). Parliamentarism Versus Semi-Presidentialism in the Baltic States: The Causes and Consequences of Differences in the Constitutional Framework. *Baltic Journal of Political Science, 2*, 7–28.

Nousiainen, J. (2001). From Semi-Presidentialism to Parliamentary Government: Political and Constitutional Developprime Ministerents in Finland. *Scandinavian Political Studies, 24*(2), 95–109.

Perju, V. (2015). The Romanian Double Executive and the 2012 Constitutional Crisis. *International Journal of Constitutional Law, 13*(1), 246–278.

Saraviita, I. (2000). *Perustuslaki 2000: Kommentaariteos uudesta valtiosäännöstä Suomelle*. Helsinki: Kauppakaari.

Urbanavičius, D. (1999). Lithuania. In R. Elgie (Ed.), *Semi-Presidentialism in Europe* (pp. 150–169). Oxford: Oxford University Press.

Urdze, S. (2016). Lithuania. In A. Fruhstorfer & M. Hein (Eds.), *Constitutional Politics in Central and Eastern Europe: From Post-Socialist Transition to the Reform of Political Systems* (pp. 439–461). Wiesbaden: Springer.

Verheijen, T. (1999). Romania. In R. Elgie (Ed.), *Semi-Presidentialism in Europe* (pp. 193–215). Oxford: Oxford University Press.

CHAPTER 5

Informal Avenues of Influence

Having investigated the existence of formal coordination devices, this chapter focuses on the various strategies and tools the president uses to shape national politics, with a particular focus on informal avenues of coordination and decision-making between the president and the prime minister. To reiterate, our main argument is that lack of written rules or otherwise strong norms guiding intra-executive coordination opens the door for presidential activism, with presidents enjoying more discretion in designing their own modes of operation. Where strong formal or de facto coordination mechanisms exist, presidents are in turn more constrained and constructively involved in decision-making. Referring to our typology of informal institutions (Chap. 2), such informal mechanisms can be either beneficial or harmful for intra-executive relations and more broadly political decision-making. Presidential activism can take many forms, from high-profile public speeches to active contacts with political parties and civil society actors, and as argued in the theoretical chapter, often such activities can undermine trust between the two leaders or facilitate presidential influence in questions falling under the competence of the government. Chapter 4 showed that Finland has considerably more intra-executive coordination mechanisms, particularly in the form of bilateral exchanges between the president and the prime minister and the foreign minister and the Ministerial Committee on Foreign and Security Policy. Lithuania and Romania have less such institutionalized cooperation instruments, and hence one should thus expect higher levels of presidential activism in Lithuania and Romania.

© The Author(s) 2020
T. Raunio, T. Sedelius, *Semi-Presidential Policy-Making in Europe*,
Palgrave Studies in Presidential Politics,
https://doi.org/10.1007/978-3-030-16431-7_5

The chapter has three empirical country sections. They follow the same structure, with each section focusing on the main question of whether the president seeks to influence policy-making in matters falling under the competence of the government (or the legislature), and if so, what strategies presidents use for that purpose. We pay special attention to the interaction between the president and political parties and the role of presidential staff. On a broader level, the chapter also examines whether presidential activism in issue areas beyond the formal powers of the presidency is perceived as legitimate and the 'appropriate course of action' in Finland, Lithuania, and Romania. The concluding discussion summarizes the findings.

5.1   FINLAND: CONSTRAINED PRESIDENCY

Toward the end of Chap. 4 we discussed the varying practices of formal coordination between our three countries and underlined the importance of the period of constitutional reform, which could in each of the cases be seen as a 'critical juncture', to use institutionalist theory terminology. In Finland the process was both calm and deliberate and based on broad consensus among the political and administrative elites about the need to constrain the president. One needs to remember that a key objective of the constitutional reform was the consolidation of parliamentary democracy. Hence not only did the drafters of the constitution pay special attention to the individual passages of the constitution, but there was also a sufficiently shared understanding among the politicians about the appropriate limits of presidential influence or actions.

This shared understanding manifests itself in a variety of ways. First, the process of government formation is purely in the hands of political parties, with the largest party (in terms of seats) leading the government formation talks after the Eduskunta elections. The last case of presidential intervention occurred in 1987, when the Social Democratic President Mauno Koivisto overruled a center-right coalition between the Centre Party and the National Coalition and appointed instead a cabinet that included the National Coalition and the Social Democrats as its two largest parties. In the twenty-first century it is expected that the president does not intervene in any way in cabinet formation (Karvonen 2016), although the president is consulted about the choice of the foreign minister. Presidents normally do not comment on ongoing government formation talks beyond perhaps expressing the hope that the talks are not delayed too much.

That presidents are not expected to intervene in government formation became evident in June 2017 when President Niinistö was criticized by many commentators on account of questioning whether the Finns Party could continue in the cabinet after it had elected member of the European Parliament Jussi Halla-aho as the new party chair. The Finns Party had been chaired for 20 years by Timo Soini who had led his party from basically zero support to scoring major electoral victories in the 2011 and 2015 Eduskunta elections. Soini had announced that he would step down as the party leader, and it was expected that another person belonging to the more moderate or populist wing of the party would succeed Soini. However, Halla-aho, who has been convicted in court for hate speech and is known for his strongly anti-immigration views, emerged victorious and also essentially all other leadership positions were now filled by the more nationalist or anti-immigrationist faction of the party. Vice-chair Teuvo Hakkarainen has also been found guilty of hate speech. Immediately following the election of Halla-aho, the two other cabinet parties, the Centre Party of Finland (KESK) and the National Coalition (KOK), ruled out the possibility of Halla-aho and his party continuing in the cabinet. The issue was solved when Soini and the more populist camp of the party left the Finns and established a new parliamentary group of their own, the Blue Reform. This enabled Soini and his colleagues to remain in the government while also ensuring that the Sipilä cabinet still controlled a majority of the Eduskunta seats. President Niinistö did not personally get involved in the negotiations between Prime Minister Sipilä and the other party leaders, but he did offer his opinion on the 'new' Finns Party: "[The party] has quite a job before them if they want to convince people that the things that led to their convictions would now vanish from the world. It would behove them to better behave themselves so that no new incidents occur again. I also haven't heard either of them distance themselves from their previous comments."[1] In another interview roughly a month later, Niinistö distanced himself from the talks: "And it wasn't really my business either. How the government negotiations would proceed and whether or not the government would seek to disband [parliament] does not fall under the president's purview."[2]

Nor do Finnish presidents criticize the governments of the day publicly. To be sure, there are differences of opinion, particularly under cohabitation, but presidents have refrained from publicly attacking the prime minister and the cabinet. The exceptions are issues falling under the foreign policy co-leadership between the president and the government, where Halonen and particularly Niinistö have on rare occasions publicly questioned the comments made by cabinet ministers. When the Social Democratic Halonen shared power with center-right prime ministers from 2003 to 2012, she often emphasized different topics in her speeches, but even in case of open clashes, such as over some civil service appointments or representation in the European Council (see Chap. 6), she did not try to delegitimize the government. Known for her leftist views and with a trade union background, Halonen had already before entering office displayed keen interest in questions of gender, equality, development policy, globalization, and the Nordic welfare state. She actively raised such themes in her election campaigns, speeches, and interviews; maintained ties with relevant civil society stakeholders; and also organized roundtable 'presidential forum' discussions about topics close to her heart. But while Halonen spoke and commented regularly about 'domestic politics', she addressed the issues mainly in more general terms without directly criticizing the government. In her New Year's speeches Halonen focused primarily on foreign and security policy, although she also talked about economy, employment, and other social issues (Hallberg et al. 2009: 346–371; Tiilikainen 2013).

President Niinistö, who was a finance minister from 1996 to 2003 and the chair of the National Coalition from 1994 to 2001, has in turn often commented on the state of the economy, both in Finland and in the European and global contexts, but such comments have mainly been rather general and not specifically directed at the government. In his official speeches Niinistö has by and large stuck to matters falling under the jurisdiction of the president, although keeping in line with his election campaigns, Niinistö has also expressed concerns about societal solidarity and growing differentiation among the population (Hämäläinen 2013). In general, Finnish presidents in their speeches and interviews primarily stick to foreign and security policy issues, thus leaving domestic politics and mainly also EU matters to the prime minister and the cabinet. Both Halonen and Niinistö have also vigilantly defended the existing constitutional prerogatives of the president.[3]

Three examples illustrate well the sensitivity of the issue and the generally held view that presidents should not intervene in domestic politics. In his 2012 presidential election campaign, Niinistö suggested that informal dialogue between the president and the government should be increased. The plan was to have informal 'evening school' sessions where current issues could be debated confidentially. Constitutional experts rejected the idea, while most of the parties emphasized that if such discussions were held, the agenda should be limited to foreign and security policy (Yli-Huttula 2018: 337). When opening the parliamentary session in February

2018, Niinistö offered to host talks about various pressing long-term issues, such as climate change, societal structures, and EU policy, but this idea was strongly rejected by the leading daily *Helsingin Sanomat* in its editorial on account of the president, thereby intruding on issues falling under the competence of the government.[4] In their book on Niinistö, two journalists Matti Mörttinen and Lauri Nurmi (2018: 243–247) revealed that the president had hosted in late 2015 a meeting between the trade union representatives and the employers' confederation. The talks were held in order to facilitate a compromise between the two sides so that the Sipilä government could move forward with its competitiveness pact (*kilpailukykysopimus*) aimed at improving the state of the economy. When accused of not respecting the constitutional division of labor between the government and the president, Niinistö clearly got agitated and defended his role by stating that he had simply hosted the meeting without even trying to influence the talks. The people present in the meeting interviewed for the book did, however, report that the president had been pushing the two sides to reach an agreement.

However, while the 'shared understanding' or the 'spirit of the constitution' might be well entrenched among the political elites, we must not lose sight of the popularity of the presidents (Chap. 3). Presidents are typically way more popular than prime ministers and other 'party politicians', and according to survey data public opinion is consistently in favor of giving the president a stronger role in politics—including in domestic politics and EU affairs. Not surprisingly, nearly all candidates in presidential elections have thus signaled that they would make active use of the powers vested in the presidency, and that they would not hesitate to comment on societally salient issues. The current president Niinistö has proven particularly trusted among the citizenry, enjoying broad support across the political spectrum. Hence, and in connection with what in the end was a very minor scandal referred to in the previous paragraph, it is telling that essentially no politician proved willing to criticize Niinistö. Furthermore, the constitution does leave the window open for presidential activism. For example, regarding government formation, the constitution simply states that the president appoints the prime minister and the other ministers after the premier has been approved by the Eduskunta. The constitution therefore does not rule out presidential interference in government formation, whereas both the dissolution of the Eduskunta and the resignation of the prime minister and the individual ministers are dependent on an initiative from the prime minister.[5]

In terms of initiating and vetoing legislation, until a constitutional amendment from 2012 the president formally delivered government bills to parliament, but in practice the president was tied to the cabinet proposal of the cabinet. From 2012 on, the president has no role in the introduction of bills. Regarding veto powers, prior to a 1987 constitutional amendment, the president could delay legislation until overridden by a newly elected Eduskunta. Between 1987 and 2000 the president could delay laws until the next parliamentary session and under the 2000 constitution this period was shortened to three months, with the parliament having the right to override the president's veto. According to the new constitution, bills adopted by the Eduskunta are submitted to the president for confirmation. If the president fails to confirm a law within three months, it is returned to the parliament. If the Eduskunta then readopts the bill 'without material alterations', it enters into force without presidential confirmation (Section 77). It must be emphasized that presidents have not challenged cabinet proposals or parliamentary decisions. Under the old constitution, and particularly during the long reign of President Kekkonen, the president had other ways of influencing government policy, whereas under the new constitution it is expected that the president does not intervene in legislative processes.

Regarding meetings with various political actors, the first thing to note is that the Finnish president stands in the Gaullist tradition firmly above party-political quarrels. When elected into office, the president resigns from her or his party. To be sure, presidents maintain some of their contacts with previous party comrades, notably to those persons closest to them, but they do not participate in any party meetings or speak at any party events outside of actual presidential election campaigns. This tradition goes to the days of the old constitution, as even then the president was expected to stay above party politics and to act, if needed, as a mediator between political parties. The president chairs the presidential sessions of the government and the Ministerial Committee on Foreign and Security Policy, but does not meet individual ministers regularly, apart from the foreign minister (see Chap. 4). The president can, however, from time to time discuss issues with other ministers and individual MPs. The president visits the Eduskunta to open the four-year legislative term and the annual parliamentary sessions, but does not meet regularly the parliamentary party groups of any of the political parties. Considering that the Foreign Affairs Committee has become closely involved in foreign and security policy and scrutinizes the government in such matters (see Chap. 6), the presidents have organized joint meetings with the committee.[6] Niinistö vowed in his 2012 election campaign to improve relations with the Eduskunta, and during his first six-year term the parliamentary committees—Foreign Affairs, Defence, Grand Committee (the EU committee), and Finance Committees—visited the president a total of 40 times. Around twice a year Niinistö also met the chairpersons of the party groups (Yli-Huttula 2018: 337). Compared with the Lithuanian and Romanian presidents, the Finnish president meets representatives of various civil society actors much less frequently. Such meetings often occur during the president's visits to various parts of the country, where the president typically attends some social event and also engages with ordinary citizens.

Finally, turning to presidential advisers, the size of the president's office is very small. According to the law, the duties of the president's office are to assist the president in carrying out official duties, to manage administration and keep the president's archive, to provide for any personal services required by the president, and to ensure the personal security of the president.[7] In late 2018 the civil service staff included the secretary general, foreign policy adviser, legal adviser, director of communications, and a special adviser. Together with the president they form the Presidential Cabinet. The presidential staff does perform an important function, not least in terms of maintaining contacts with the prime minister's office and the foreign ministry. Yet it is clear that the president is strongly dependent on the preparatory work carried out by the government.

5.2   Lithuania: Presidents Stamping Their Authority

In Lithuania and Romania the situation is very different indeed. In these two cases the analysis centers more around individual office-holders. It highlights the importance of personalities, with presidents enjoying considerable discretion in shaping their relations with other state institutions. Most of the interviewed persons in both countries confirmed that each president brings her own communication and inter-institutional coordination style. However, the influence of the respective certainly is also dependent on party politics, with cohabitation producing more intra-executive tensions.

Since democratization Lithuania has had four presidents, Brazauskas, Adamkus, Grybauskaitė, and Paksas, but we limit our analysis essentially to the first here given that the presidency of Paksas was so short-lived (see Chap. 3). Previous research has described the first office-holder Brazauskas as a constructive leader. He upheld the position as head of state carefully without open conflicts with the prime minister or the Seimas. One of his former advisers noted that Brazauskas was careful not to antagonize the government or the Seimas, and hence had regular meetings with the other main political leaders. He was referred to as a 'housekeeper' who wanted to ensure that his country was functioning properly. While Brazauskas was very much a party politician, he was also a key figure in the transition to democracy and remained popular throughout his political career, including from 2001 to 2006 as the prime minister (see below). Brazauskas also favored an open style of leadership, including active contacts with ordinary citizens. Interestingly his staff comprised mainly of policy advisers in areas falling under the competence of the government (social policy, economic policy, education, science, culture and religion, sports, municipalities, information, health care). Their task was to analyze documents approved by the parliament and the government, to follow important developments, and to formulate proposals for the president. In addition, Brazauskas used decrees to establish various commissions and councils on topics like state defense, foreign policy, citizenship, culture, fighting organized crime, and judicial reform. He also utilized a Political Consultation Council for domestic matters, the membership of which included representatives of the major parties and prominent figures from science, art, and education. While much of this activity can be explained by the real need to address serious societal issues facing the young democracy, it also probably influenced the choices made by his successors.

Brazauskas (2007: 70) himself noted that as the constitutional powers of the president are limited, he tried to influence the Seimas and the government with his 'political authority' and support of the people. This was easier during the first four years of the presidency when his party LDDP was in government and controlled the parliamentary majority. Upon entering office, he wanted 'first of all' to form a relationship with the Seimas. An important factor here was good relations with the Seimas' leadership, with Brazauskas also meeting the main party groups and individual MPs, especially to discuss his legislative initiatives. Obviously his contacts were more frequent with LDDP, the party he had chaired before winning the presidency. However, following the 1996 Seimas elections things got more difficult for Brazauskas under the center-right coalition of Homeland Union and Christian Democrats (TS-LKD), and the president essentially limited his actions to the sphere of foreign affairs. Brazauskas faced difficulties in establishing contacts with the ruling coalition, and while he met

Prime Minister Gediminas Vagnorius (Homeland Union) regularly, the latter emphasized the need to respect the jurisdictional limits set by the constitution. In his memoirs Brazauskas (2007: 82) observed that during the period of more than a year of cohabitation, the prime minister 'had never given a phone call' to the president.

Adamkus came from a very different background, having served in the Environmental Protection Agency of the United States for nearly two decades. Elected on an independent ticket both in the 1998 and in the 2004 presidential elections, Adamkus (2004: 38) wrote that he needed to 'create traditions' for the institution of the president. Adamkus' team of advisers clearly wielded strong influence in presidential decision-making, particularly during his first term. Having observed the weak position of Brazauskas toward the end of his presidency, Adamkus wanted to act as 'counterweight' to the government and not let parties impose their own will on him. In 1999, a severe conflict occurred between Adamkus and Prime Minister Vagnorius when the president openly criticized Vagnorius about economic reform. As the president had no friendly majority in the Seimas, he leaned on his popular support. Opinion polls at the time showed approval rates of over 80 percent for the president, and less than 20 percent for the prime minister (Sedelius 2006: 149). Adamkus publicly voiced his distrust in the prime minister and stated that he could not perform his presidential duties as long as Vagnorius stayed on the post. The sharp decline of the economy, following the Russian economic crisis, gave the president the upper hand and he could effectively insist—although without formal dismissal powers—on the resignation of Vagnorius. The fact that Vagnorius chose to step down was an important moment in strengthening presidential leadership.

Adamkus would not limit his scope of activities to foreign and security policy. In fact, already during his presidential election campaign Adamkus declared his intention of reforming the tax system (Urbanavičius 1999: 166). With his team he would try to influence 'governmental issues', particularly budgets but also agriculture, or the privatization of oil refinery *Mazeikiu nafta*. At the start of his first term Adamkus took steps to consolidate his foreign policy leadership and did not hesitate to disagree with the foreign minister even though public confrontations were largely avoided. He also abolished the Ministry for European Affairs and took an active role in coordinating EU affairs. Following Lithuania joining the EU in 2004, Adamkus participated in the European Council mainly when foreign policy was on the agenda. Otherwise the prime minister represented

Lithuania or both executives attended the summits. Adamkus had regular bilateral meetings with all prime ministers, with such meetings usually held upon the initiative of the president. The agendas of the meetings covered all types of societal issues, from economy to foreign affairs to problems inside the government. However, when Brazauskas was the prime minister from 2001 to 2006, his advisers saw that there was little interest from Adamkus and the president's office to genuinely communicate and cooperate with the government. Adamkus also actively consulted the speaker of the Seimas, the leaders of parliamentary groups, individual ministers, or key civil servants, not least when the governing coalition seemed not to be operating effectively.

It appears that during his second term Adamkus adopted overall a less assertive stance, with the balance of power more in favor of the prime minister even during the minority government of Kirgilas (2006–2008). Adamkus faced prime ministers and cabinets from opposing political camps most of the period. Support ratings also mattered, as Brazauskas was also during his premiership an unusually popular politician in Lithuania. In addition, the political scandal surrounding Paksas' impeachment called for a less confrontational approach in order to rebuild confidence in the political system in general and in the presidency in particular. Nonetheless, in 2006 Adamkus again resorted to a statement on national television questioning whether the government still enjoyed the confidence of the Seimas, with Prime Minister Brazauskas resigning afterward. And in 2005 Adamkus had intervened in the conflicts between Viktor Uspaskich, the leader of the Labour Party and the minister of economic affairs, and Artūras Zuokas, the mayor of Vilnius and the chair of the Liberal and Centre Union. In another television appearance, Adamkus requested that the quarreling politicians resign from their public offices, with Uspaskich indeed deciding to leave his ministerial post.

By all accounts, President Grybauskaitė, also elected as an independent candidate in both the 2009 and the 2014 elections (although in 2009 she was supported by the center-right parties Homeland Union-Lithuanian Christian Democrats and the Liberal Movement) became more powerful than her predecessors. Throughout her tenure in office her leadership style has been characterized as assertive and confrontational. With the exception of the 2009–2012 period, Grybauskaitė has shared power with premiers from opposing camps, and this has no doubt influenced her behavioral strategies. Grybauskaitė's team of advisers followed the governmental agenda closely according to their spheres of competence, and again the advisers covered issues outside of presidential jurisdiction (economic and social policy, national security, education, science and culture, legal affairs, interior policy, foreign policy). Grybauskaitė met the prime minister weekly, and all of these meetings as well as meetings with other ministers were publicly announced, but as mentioned in Chap. 4, in spring 2016 Grybauskaitė stopped having these meetings with Prime Minister Butkevičius, and for almost six months there were no regular working meetings with the prime minister. Presidential advisers had regular contacts with relevant ministries and the prime minister's office. Advisers took part in the sittings of the government, expressing, if needed, the position of the president. Perhaps more importantly, they kept track of the preparatory work carried out in the ministries, trying at least occasionally to influence decision-making already before a draft proposal was discussed in the cabinet. Grybauskaitė and her team also approached other stakeholders such as civil society actors.

As explained in more detail in Chap. 6, in foreign and security policy the president obviously had more direct ways of influencing policy-making. Her influence appeared also strong in EU and economic affairs, partly because she had served previously as the finance minister and as the Commissioner for Financial Programming and the Budget. Grybauskaitė has shown special interest in various economic questions, from taxes to pensions reform. Here the political context favored her assertiveness. The economic crisis preoccupied the already weak cabinet led by Prime Minister Kubilius (2008–2012), with Grybauskaitė supporting the government while increasing her own authority. Examining four key policy reforms—civil service reform, higher education reform, restructuring of personal health-care organizations, and pension reform—initiated by the Kubilius cabinet, Nakrošis et al. (2018) show how presidential support or acquiescence was important for the adoption of the proposed measures. This applied particularly to civil service reform. After the plan had been strongly criticized by the parliamentary opposition and some members of the ruling Homeland Union, Grybauskaitė in a bilateral meeting with Kubilius expressed her disapproval of the reform, following which the government withdrew the reform bill.

However, from late 2012 to 2016, Grybauskaitė shared power with the Social Democratic-led coalition of Butkevičius, and then from 2016 onward with the cabinet led by Prime Minister Saulius Skvernelis that brought together the Farmers and Greens Union and the Social Democrats. By 2018 the relations between Grybauskaitė and Skvernelis had soured over various disputes. Grybauskaitė was on particularly bad terms with the chair of the Farmers and Greens Union, Ramūnas Karbauskis. Interestingly, in her State of the Nation address in the Seimas in June 2018, the president focused on the ongoing corruption scandals, but also unleashed a strong attack on the government and the legislature for failing to address major societal problems, while simultaneously calling on the main political actors to stop all the warring in the name of Lithuania's national interest. Such a move needs to be understood in the context of the 'email-gate affair', which had at least temporarily impacted on the public image of the president.[8] In September Grybauskaitė invited the prime minister, the speaker of the Seimas, and the leaders of the two largest parties for an informal dinner at the presidential palace. Karbauskis declined the invitation and Grybauskaitė called the dinner off (Park 2018a, b). There were also serious jurisdictional disputes about relations with Russia that will be discussed in more detail in Chap. 6.

All presidents have intervened in the life cycle of governments. As in Finland, the constitution leaves room for interpretation regarding the role of the president in government formation, as according to Section 84(4), the president "shall, upon the assent of the Seimas, appoint the Prime Minister; shall charge the Prime Minister with forming the Government; and shall approve the composition of the formed Government".[9] The president also releases the prime minister from her or his duties upon assent of the Seimas and, following an initiative from the prime minister, shall appoint and fire individual ministers. As previous literature has examined this question in careful detail (Matsuzato and Gudžinskas 2006; Krupavičius 2008, 2013; Norkus 2013), select examples are only provided here. There is an 'unwritten agreement' that the president has a say on who will be appointed as ministers of foreign affairs and defense regardless of the ideological color of the government. However, presidents have regularly also either handpicked individual prime ministers or especially rejected candidates for other portfolios. Brazauskas without prior consultations nominated Adolfas Šleževičius as the prime minister in 1993, only to replace him with another ex-communist Mindaugas Stankevičius in 1996. Adamkus deliberately undermined the position of Prime Minister Vagnorius, including through a high-profile television speech in which he declared his lack of trust in Vagnorius, and managed to get Paksas appointed as his successor in 1999. In fact, in late 2000 Adamkus chose the leader of the Liberal Union of Lithuania (LLS) Paksas to form a 'new politics' government despite the fact that the Social Democratic coalition led by Brazauskas had won the elections. And when the cabinet was suffering from internal turmoil in 2006, Adamkus again used a public television speech to enforce the resignation of Prime Minister Brazauskas. Interestingly, in 2004 Adamkus met the president of the Constitutional Court, Egidijus Kuris, to discuss how to proceed if the preferences of the prime minister and the president regarding ministerial candidates differed. According to Kuris the constitution offered no direct solutions, thus paving the way for presidential activism.

Grybauskaitė in turn enforced in 2010 the resignation of Vygaudas Ušackas, the foreign minister. In 2012 she refused to appoint as ministers several well-known politicians and even tried to exclude the Labour Party from the government.[10] Grybauskaitė has made it clear that she pays special attention to the competence of the minister of finance. In 2014 after her re-election Grybauskaitė had no choice but to confirm Butkevičius as the prime minister, but she announced that she would not reappoint other cabinet ministers unless they sacked deputy ministers that had appeared on a 'black list' of people with suspicious financial activities. Constitutionally the president has no such dismissal powers, but in the end the government agreed to fire the deputy ministers (Köker 2014b). After the 2016 elections Grybauskaitė made it clear that she intends to shape the selection of ministers. In the spring of 2018 she enforced the resignation of the Minister of Agriculture Bronius Markauskas and rejected Prime Minister Skvernelis' candidate for the minister for justice.

Presidents have also made fairly active use of their power to veto legislation. Article 71 of the constitution gives the president the right to send, "upon reasonable grounds" and within ten days, bills back to the Seimas for reconsideration. The Seimas can override presidential vetoes with an absolute majority of its members. The Seimas can also, in line with Article 72, adopt changes proposed by the president with a simple majority, making it thus easier for the legislature to accept presidential proposals than to override the veto. Between 1992 and 2010 Lithuanian presidents vetoed 175 bills, 3 percent of all laws introduced in that period, with President Grybauskaitė also vetoing bills during her first term. However, a closer examination of the vetoes suggests that a sizeable share of them were 'constructive' vetoes, with Grybauskaitė in her so-called amendatory observations primarily pointing out various legal problems in the initiatives. Moreover, the Lithuanian presidents also enjoy the power of legislative initiative. Between 1992 and 2010, Lithuanian presidents tabled close to 1 percent of all legislative initiatives (Köker 2014a, 2017).

Lithuanian presidents clearly have not hesitated to 'go public', often questioning the legitimacy of prime ministers and their governments. Without any constitutional powers to dismiss the prime minister, President Adamkus used high-profile television speeches to force Prime Ministers Vagnorius and Brazauskas to resign, while President Grybauskaitė has on several occasions criticized both the government and individual ministers.[11] Obviously a large part of presidential speeches and interviews are held in connection with visits abroad or hosting foreign leaders, but Lithuanian presidents have routinely also commented on matters falling under the competence of the government.[12] Interestingly, Article 84(18) of the Lithuanian constitution specifically dictates that the president "shall make annual reports at the Seimas on the situation in Lithuania and the domestic and foreign policies of the Republic of Lithuania". In such a 'State of the Nation Address' in April 2001, President Adamkus attacked the Paksas cabinet: "there are not many signs of a new style in the work of the parliament, in relations between Seimas and the Cabinet, and altogether of new … politics. Parties of the coalition are not strong. So far they obviously lack an experience in governance, a direction and continuity in actions" (Krupavičius 2013: 224). President Grybauskaitė has essentially in all her State of the Nation addresses criticized the government or the Lithuanian political system at large.

But we must at the same time emphasize that all office-holders have understood that coordination between the three main state institutions—the president, the government, and the Seimas—is necessary as no actor can alone achieve anything. Thus, presidents maintain working relations with the governing coalition, individual ministers, party leaders, and the sectoral committees of the Seimas. Discussions are held in order to avoid conflicts and even in the event of a (public) disagreement both sides try to build a compromise. Overall, the frequency of contacts and the smoothness of cooperation have depended partly on party-political dynamics, but here we must remember that both Adamkus and Grybauskaitė were elected as independent candidates. Also constitutionally the president stands above parties: according to Article 83 of the Lithuanian constitution, "a person elected the President of the Republic must suspend his activities in political parties and political organisations until the beginning of a new campaign for the election of the President of the Republic". Respective communication officers from the offices of the prime minister and the president coordinate their activities to ensure that potential disagreements do not surface, particularly in foreign and security policy.

Again, this cooperation is not based on any written rules: the goal is simply to inform one another of developments and of forthcoming speeches or press releases.

The presidential staff has performed a key role in facilitating presidential activism and also policy influence. As the preceding analysis shows, the staff of each Lithuanian president has comprised also or even mainly policy advisers in areas falling under the competence of the government—including social policy, economic policy, education, culture, religion, and so on. In late 2018 the office of President Grybauskaitė brought together 50 persons under the following organizational headings: Economic and Social Policy Group (8 advisers), National Security Group (4), Press Service (11), Education, Science and Culture Group (5), Legal Affairs Group (5), Domestic Policy Group (2), Foreign Policy Group (10, four of whom work for the Protocol Division), and the Office of the Chancellor (5). With the help of these advisors, successive presidents have actively formed ties with not just individual ministers and ministries but also political parties, the speakers, party groups and individual deputies of the Seimas, and civil society stakeholders. The high number of communication officers also deserves attention, as it indicates both the overall importance of the presidency in Lithuanian politics and an active dialogue with the media.

Overall, we can thus see a clear difference to the Finnish case: in Lithuania it is perceived by and large legitimate and appropriate for the president to become involved in domestic politics. Presidents have stamped their authority throughout the period under analysis, and presidents have also emerged victorious from most intra-executive battles. Brazauskas may have been a constructive 'statesman', respectful of the constitutional division of labor between the two executives, but already set the example by maintaining active contacts with other state institutions and civil society actors and by intervening in issues in the jurisdiction of the government. Indeed, the analysis shows quite substantial continuity since the early 1990s. Like in other semi-presidential regimes, periods of cohabitation reduce the influence of the president and result in more intra-executive disputes. At other times, such as when Grybauskaitė entered office in 2009, the economic and political conditions can facilitate very assertive presidential behavior. Presidents have also benefited from their popularity, with Adamkus and Grybauskaitė further reinforcing this through their anti-party or anti-establishment rhetoric (Krupavičius 2013). Regardless of such factors, the roughly quarter of century of semi-presidentialism indicates that it is legitimate for Lithuanian presidents to step beyond their constitutional powers and intervene in questions falling under the competence of the government or the Seimas.

5.3   Romania: When Mediation Goes Too Far

Largely the same applies to Romania, where we also see notable variation between individual presidents. Two presidents, Ion Iliescu (1990–1996, 2000–2004) and Traian Băsescu (2004–2014), were noted for their high level of activism and willingness to challenge the government, whereas Presidents Emil Constantinescu (1996–2000) and Klaus Iohannis (2014–) have adopted more cautious modes of operation. Overall, cohabitation has clearly mattered more in Romania than in Finland or Lithuania, with the activist presidents also utilizing party contacts to a larger extent than in our other two cases.

To understand the role of political parties in facilitating or hindering presidential activism, it is essential to go back to the early 1990s when Romania was drafting its first democratic constitution. In the debates about the presidency, Iliescu did not seem that bothered with the exact constitutional prerogatives of the institution. Instead, he prioritized concurrent presidential and parliamentary elections. The inspiration came very much from France, where presidential influence is mainly achieved through a friendly parliamentary majority and avoiding cohabitation. Iliescu thus calculated (correctly) that concurrent elections would result in the same party or coalition capturing both the presidency and the legislative majority and the post of the prime minister. Another significant element inspired by the French experience was having the president to act as a mediator between the other key national political institutions. Thus according to Article 80(2) of the constitution, "the President of Romania shall guard the observance of the Constitution and the proper functioning of the public authorities. To this effect, he shall act as a mediator between the Powers in the State, as well as between the State and society" (Elgie 2018: 215–249; Verheijen 1999; Tănăsescu 2008; Guţan 2012; Perju 2015).

Iliescu had been a very powerful and popular figure during the transition to democracy, and this clearly facilitated his activism in office. Iliescu intervened regularly in the affairs of his party and used the party for his own purposes. This was not difficult, as the NSF/Social Democrats were very much a dominant actor in Romanian politics and economy until the mid-1990s. With the cabinet of Prime Minister Petre Roman faring badly in the polls on account of its economic reforms, Iliescu most likely orchestrated a miners' strike in the fall of 1991 to force the resignation of Roman who had been fighting for influence with Iliescu inside the party. Iliescu and Roman disagreed about several issues, from how to react to the coup in Russia (see Chap. 6) to the broader democratization and modernization process in Romania. After ousting Roman, Iliescu secured the appointment of two loyal prime ministers, Theodor Stolojan and Nicolae Văcăroiu. Iliescu was clearly using his links to a variety of stakeholders, from trade unions to big businesses to the intelligence services, and even publicly criticized many court decisions. Corruption was rife, and by many accounts the president was deeply involved in it. The year 1994 also saw an impeachment procedure against Iliescu on account of the president not respecting the division of duties between state institutions, especially regarding courts. The Constitutional Court saw that Iliescu's public statements did not constitute "grave acts infringing upon Constitutional provisions" (as required by Article 95 of the constitution), and also the friendly parliamentary majority voted against impeachment. By the time Iliescu returned to the presidency in 2000, Romania had taken steps toward a more democratic society and was approaching EU membership. Iliescu displayed more restraint during his second period in office, but there were nonetheless rather persistent tensions with Prime Minister Adrian Năstase, again from his own Social Democratic Party, in part because Năstase was in favor of amending the constitution to reduce presidential powers.

Like Iliescu, President Băsescu had considerable experience from power struggles and party politics before entering office. Former captain of an oil tanker, he had served as minister of transport in several cabinets during the 1990s, as well as four years as the mayor of Bucharest. Băsescu certainly did not shy away from confrontations with the governments and used a variety of channels to influence Romanian politics. In the 2004 parliamentary elections the Social Democrats emerged as the largest party, but President Băsescu instead appointed as the Prime Minister Călin Popescu-Tăriceanu from the National Liberal Party which was in an alliance together with Băsescu's Democratic Party. Furthermore, Băsescu was able to persuade the Humanist Party to break their pre-electoral coalition with the Social Democrats and to join the new government. This way Băsescu managed to avoid cohabitation while also achieving a friendly majority in the legislature. Băsescu's position was so strong that he basically even "handpicked some of the ministers" (Anghel 2018b: 111). However, by the end of

2006 the Humanists left the coalition and the relations between the two leaders had become tense. Băsescu wanted to topple Popescu-Tăriceanu, who fired the Democratic Party ministers from his cabinet, but the latter refused to resign. Băsescu publicly attacked the government, alluding to various shady, mafia-type economic interests influencing its work, while unleashing similar criticism at the Social Democrats, which by now was supporting the government. In a public speech Băsescu accused Prime Minister Popescu-Tăriceanu of asking the president to intervene in favor of Dinu Patriciu, a member of the Liberal party who had been caught in a corruption case. Băsescu even presented pieces of his private conversation with Popescu-Tăriceanu in a press conference that was covered widely by the media (Gherghina et al. 2016: 12). Hence began the difficult cohabitation period between Băsescu and the Popescu-Tăriceanu cabinet now consisting of the Liberals and the Democratic Alliance of Hungarians in Romania (UDMR). For example, according to the comparative study of Elgie (2018: 127–149), this cohabitation produced one of the highest levels of intra-executive conflict across the examined 21 European countries.

Following the 2008 parliamentary elections, Băsescu, using a discourse related to the global financial crisis, called for the formation of a grand coalition between the Liberal Democratic Party (PDL) and the PSD (together they had won more than two-thirds of the seats). This coalition lasted until October 2009 when the Social Democrats left the coalition. Two months later, Băsescu was re-elected as president by a very narrow margin and was able to forge a legislative majority for his party (PDL) with the help of the UDMR and using 35 defector MPs from the PSD and the Liberals. As in 2004, Băsescu influenced strongly the formation of the Boc government. From 2008 to 2011 Băsescu's position was indeed very strong and this period probably was the peak in the 'presidentialization' of Romanian politics so far. According to Anghel (2017: 24), "Although [Băsescu] did not attend the coalition meetings, he held close contact with his loyal Prime Minister Emil Boc. Members of the Boc cabinets testified that the president was in a position of great strength and had the power to overturn decisions taken by the coalition." However, by early 2012 the government's popularity was sinking fast on account of austerity measures. Băsescu reacted by changing the prime minister from Boc to technocrat Mihai Răzvan Ungureanu. The PDL did not appreciate this move, as many inside the party felt that the replacement of the prime minister had been decided alone by the president. Following the successful motion of no confidence in April 2012 against the Ungureanu cabinet, Băsescu was forced to appoint the Social Democrat Victor Ponta as the new prime minister.

Another example of Băsescu's activism, although one that was based on the constitutional powers invested in the presidency, came in connection with the 2009 presidential elections. According to Article 90 of the constitution, the president "may, after consultation with Parliament, ask the people of Romania to express, by referendum, their will on matters of national interest". Băsescu, whose popularity had declined, engaged in his campaigns in a strong discourse about state modernization, arguing that existing political institutions were inefficient. Băsescu thus used his constitutional right and called for two consultative referendums on introducing a single-chamber legislature and lowering the number of MPs to 300. Both referenda were passed with strong majorities in favor of the president's positions, and subsequently the issues were linked to a larger constitutional reform that also enjoyed the support of the government led by Prime Minister Boc. However, by 2011 when the constitutional reform bill was presented to the parliament, the ruling president-friendly coalition was in trouble and had no way of achieving the required two-thirds majorities in both chambers. In the end the bill was voted down in May 2013 under the leadership of the new Ponta II cabinet (Gherghina and Hein 2016: 185–186).

However, it was exactly this activism which led to the two impeachment cases against Băsescu. Behind both impeachments was his alleged misuse of presidential powers, especially the way he overstepped the 'mediating' function prescribed in the constitution. Băsescu was argued to have interfered unnecessarily in the work of the government and the legislature and to have used his party connections in an unconstitutional manner, and in 2012 he was also accused of violating the independence of the courts while there was also a serious dispute about who represents Romania in the European Council (see Chap. 6). As further evidence of his confrontational style, Băsescu also unleashed strong attacks against the media. Furthermore, Băsescu repeatedly called for a constitutional amendment that would have enabled the president to dissolve the parliament. In its ruling from 2012, the Constitutional Court dismissed the charges against the president as falling short of "grave acts against the constitution" within the meaning of Article 95 of the constitution. At the same time the court criticized President Băsescu for his failure to be neutral and to act as a 'mediator' in society. In the 2007 referendum 74.5 percent of the voters were against impeachment. In 2012, 89 percent voted for the impeachment, but the turnout at 46 percent was below the required threshold. Particularly in 2012 there was also strong pressure from the EU to solve the crisis and for Prime Minister Ponta to achieve the court ruling (Gherghina and Miscoiu 2013; Iusmen 2015; Perju 2015).

Hence Băsescu emerged in the end victorious from both impeachment cases, but obviously such serious disputes do leave scars. For instance, in 2012, after the Social Liberal Union had won the parliamentary elections with a comfortable majority, Prime Minister Ponta and President Băsescu entered a 'cohabitation pact', officially titled 'Agreement on Institutional Collaboration between the President of Romania and the Prime Minister of the Government'.[13] Its main purpose was to send a positive signal to international institutions regarding Romanian decision-makers' commitment to avoiding further political deadlock: "The institutional cooperation agreement is aimed at keeping the country stability and ensuring a functional climate for a good governance and ensuring the confidence of international markets, through harmonization of joint positions within the Executive power, with observance of the constitutional powers of the Romanian President and Government". The pact outlined a division of competencies with presidential leadership in foreign affairs in exchange for the government's pre-eminence in domestic economic and social matters: "President: foreign policy, security, defense, representation at the European Council according to the CCR Decision. Prime minister: Economic and social governance of the country, current issues which do not involve national security, external relations at European and intergovernmental levels."[14] However, by 2013 the pact seemed already forgotten and old habits returned (Gherghina et al. 2016: 17). Nonetheless, given that the Ponta II cabinet enjoyed strong majorities in both chambers of the parliament, Băsescu had little choice but to accept a more limited role during the final two years of his presidency.

Presidents Constantinescu and Iohannis have behaved in much less confrontational manner, but also they have not been spared of intra-executive tensions. Constantinescu had finished second in the 1992 presidential elections, but his background was more in academia and in civil society activism. Before being elected as the president Constantinescu had chaired the anti-communist coalition Democratic Convention, but this was really more of an umbrella alliance of various forces aiming to distance Romania from its socialist past. Constantinescu's presidency was characterized by considerable societal challenges, from societal unrest to economic decline, while trying to consolidate democracy and a stronger administration in order to edge closer toward both EU and NATO memberships. Constantinescu shared power with three premiers—Victor Ciorbea (1996–1998, Christian Democratic-National Peasants' Party), Radu Vasile (1998–1999, Christian Democratic-National Peasants Party), and Mugur Isărescu (1999–2000, independent). As already described in Chap. 3, in 1999 Constantinescu tried to oust Prime Minister Vasile from office. The Vasile cabinet was suffering from internal disputes and poor economic performance. In a bilateral conversation Constantinescu asked Vasile to resign, but as the latter refused to comply, the president then asked all other ministers to step down. The ministers obeyed Constantinescu, who then issued a presidential decree in which he sacked Vasile. Aware that the president had no such constitutional instrument, Vasile first refused to resign but finally gave in to pressure. Constantinescu's maneuver also seemed to have the support of the main political parties. As a result of this incidence, the constitution (Article 107) was reformed in 2003 to avoid any interpretation that the president is entitled to dismiss the prime minister. However, as concluded by Perju (2015: 253), overall Constantinescu preferred not to intervene in domestic matters: "Constantinescu's view of the proper role of the head of state as a detached, above-the-politics statesman led him to focus on foreign affairs and rarely interfere in his government's domestic policies."

Klaus Iohannis in turn had served as a mayor of a small town in Transylvania and was noted for his civil society activism, particularly regarding Germans in Romania. Iohannis had led the National Liberal Party for half a year before being elected as the president, but like Constantinescu, he lacked the kind of party politics background that Iliescu and Băsescu possessed. Overall, Iohannis maintained a rather loose connection to his party. His term was plagued by the continuing instability of Romanian politics, including corruption charges against leading politicians, court cases, various political scandals, and of course profound distrust in the political elite. Iohannis has therefore co-ruled with several prime ministers: Victor Ponta (Social Democrat, 2012–2015), Dacian Cioloș (independent leading a technocrat government, November 2015–January 2017), Sorin Grindeanu (Social Democrat, January–June 2017), Mihai Tudose (Social Democrat, June 2017–January 2018), and Viorica Dăncilă (Social Democrat, January 2018–).

Elected on the basis of an anti-corruption campaign, Iohannis has mainly clashed with the government over corruption. Iohannis has constantly criticized the various cabinets for not tackling the problems and has refused to appoint politicians with links to corruption to public positions. On 18 January 2017, Iohannis attended unexpectedly a meeting of the Grindeanu cabinet that discussed an emergency decree to pardon certain detainees and amend the penal code. Four days later the president joined street protests against the planned government ordinance. Iohannis then announced that he would call a referendum should the government not withdraw the bill. Iohannis has also intervened in government formation and termination. During 2015 tensions between Iohannis and Prime Minister Ponta surfaced repeatedly, with the president questioning governmental key policies, including a new fiscal plan, and calling for Ponta to resign after a criminal investigation opened against him. Following the resignation of Prime Minister Ponta in the middle of nation-wide anti-corruption protests in November 2015, Iohannis nominated the former EU Commissioner for Agriculture, Cioloș as the new premier. In December 2016 Iohannis refused to nominate Sevil Shhaideh as the prime minister without publicly explaining the reasons behind his decision. The Social Democratic Alliance of Liberals and Democrats coalition responded by threatening with presidential impeachment. Iohannis subsequently appointed the second nominee of the Social Democrats, Grindeanu, as the prime minister. In early January 2017 Iohannis delivered a sharp attack at the government in a speech held on the occasion of the Grindeanu cabinet taking office. Iohannis criticized the government for not specifying how it would tackle the budgetary deficit while also promising to increase salaries and pensions and cut down value-added tax (Bucur 2017). In March 2017 the parliament retaliated by adopting a declaration accusing Iohannis of interfering in executive-legislative relations.

In the spring of 2018 Iohannis ran into serious cooperation problems with Prime Minister Dăncilă, which peaked over a decision to move the country's embassy in Israel. After Dăncilă had repeatedly avoided meetings and phone conversations on both domestic and international issues with Iohannis, the president asked Dăncilă to resign, arguing that "she can't cope with the role of prime minister of Romania and is transforming the government into a vulnerability". Iohannis also accused Dăncilă of taking orders from her political party, announcing that the prime minister no longer enjoyed his confidence and that the Dăncilă cabinet should resign.[15] Iohannis repeated his call in November 2018, this time referring to the need to manage the approaching EU presidency (see Chap. 6). According to Iohannis it was a "political necessity" to replace the government, which he called a "crash of Romanian democracy".[16] However, despite such intra-executive conflicts and public appearances calling for the governments to resign, Iohannis has nonetheless been more reserved in his use of informal channels of influence than Băsescu.

An examination of the key 'commitments' listed on the presidential website clearly shows that the policy ambitions of Iohannis extend to domestic matters. Apart from foreign policy and defense and national security, the list includes rule of law and reform of political institutions, President Klaus Iohannis' Country Project, Educated Romania, Health, and Romanians Abroad. The commitment to 'rule of law and reform of political institutions' suggests the mediating function of the president, whereas in the 'country project' the goal is to achieve a modern and prosperous Romania. For that end, a Presidential Commission, bringing together representatives from the political parties and the civil society, "has been created to elaborate the Country Project with the purpose to debate and provide guidelines to develop and modernize Romania, as well as to draft a programmatic political document meant to reach a consensus of the parliamentary parties and political fractions".[17] While all the 'commitments' are framed in rather general terms, they provide further evidence of the many channels through which Romanian presidents can try to influence issues in the competence of the government.

Romanian presidents use fairly routinely the 'going public' strategy, blaming the government for various policy failures and commenting on issues under the jurisdiction of the cabinet. The majority of presidential speeches are widely covered by the media and the public is quite attentive. An interesting feature in this regard is the presidential speeches in the parliament. According to Article 88, "the President of Romania shall address Parliament by messages on the main political issues of the nation". Such messages have become more numerous over time and can be considered as an agenda-setting device, with the president presenting his vision about the most important societal questions. Such vision is more likely to be implemented if the president has a friendly majority in the legislature, whereas under cohabitation the president criticizes governmental decisions and tries to promote his own views on how Romania should be governed. Between December 2014 and March 2016 Iohannis addressed MPs six times, whereas Constantinescu (1996–2000) addressed MPs only once, Iliescu during his second time in office (2000–2004) five times, and Băsescu 17 times between 2004 and 2011 (Levai and Tomescu 2012; Bucur 2016).[18]

The 'going public' strategy can also be used in connection with veto powers, as the admittedly unusual episode of Iohannis joining street protests shows. According to Article 77 of the constitution, the president may send the bill back to the parliament for reconsideration or may refer it to the Constitutional Court to check its conformity with the constitution. In case the president sends the bill back to the parliament, the MPs can readopt it with a simple majority. Between 2004 and 2010 President Băsescu vetoed just over 1 percent of the bills while sending 0.1 percent to judicial review (Köker 2017). From 2015 to February 2018, President Iohannis in turn vetoed 3 percent of bills, with the parliament in most cases amending the bills before adopting them again (Anghel 2018a).

The size of the president's office is considerably larger than in Finland or Lithuania, and the advisors to the president cover essentially all policy sectors. Apart from the President's Cabinet and the General Secretariat, in late 2018 the presidential administration was divided into the following departments: National Security; Foreign Policy; European Affairs; Legislative Affairs; Relations with Public Authorities and Civil Society; Domestic Politics; Institutional and Constitutional Reform; Economic and Social Policies; Culture, Religion, and Centenary; Public Health; Education and Research; Relation with Romanians Abroad; Public Communication; and Protocol. Each department is headed by a presidential advisor and has roughly three to five employees who essentially come and go with each president. Altogether around 200 persons work for the president. As in Lithuania, the titles of the departments and their publicly stated functions indicate that the policy ambitions of the president extend to issue areas in the jurisdiction of the government. These staff members follow developments in their policy areas and communicate the president's positions to the government, the legislature, and the political parties, and maintain links with politicians and civil society stakeholders. The generous size of the staff is under the right circumstances a formidable resource for the Romanian president.

The clearest difference between Romania, on the one hand, and Finland and Lithuania, on the other hand, is in the role of political parties. Romanian presidents, and particularly Băsescu and Iliescu, have not hesitated to make active use of their political parties or friendly ruling coalitions for achieving their policy goals. Băsescu was effectively leading his Democratic Party while in office. According to Article 84 of the constitution, "During his term of office, the President of Romania may not be a member of any political party, nor may he perform any other public or private office". Yet apart from the presidents working through their parties, they have also attended party congresses and other events of their political parties and have influenced selection of party leaders. Presidents have also become directly involved in electoral campaigning. According to Gherghina et al. (2016: 14–15), this practice was started by the Social Democrats in the 2004 elections, but peaked really in the 2014 elections during the last days of Băsescu's presidency. After Băsescu had failed to get his loyal supporter Elena Udrea nominated as the new leader of PDL, the president declared his intention of establishing a new right-wing political movement. Băsescu publicly supported the creation of the Popular Movement Party (PMP), with the president appearing in the media wearing a T-shirt with the slogan 'Vote for PMP'. Prime Minister Ponta asked the Constitutional Court to determine whether Băsescu had breached the constitution, but Băsescu simply replied, "he is entitled to wear whatever clothes he wishes", adding that he shall vote for the PMP. Already in the 2007 European Parliament elections, the Democratic Party used Băsescu's popularity. The Democratic Party posters carried pictures of all the candidates, but in the middle of the poster was a large open space on which a caption read 'busy elsewhere' (Tănăsescu 2008). As summarized by Anghel (2018b: 102): "Although legally considered to shed political *parti pris* once in office, the president's bias towards his or her party of origin is expected."[19]

The last concurrent presidential and parliamentary elections were held in 2004, and subsequent elections have—as predicted—brought about more instances of cohabitation. Until then the parliamentary and presidential elections had been held simultaneously (1992, 1996, and 2000), with the result that the same coalition or party had always captured both the presidency and the position of the prime minister. The idea of the constitutional change from 2003 was thus to strengthen the checks and balances in the Romanian political system (Gherghina and Hein 2016). During periods of cohabitation the role of the president has been much more limited, whereas under unified government presidents have wielded strong influence through their parties. But checks and balances have also resulted in more severe intra-executive battles, including the two impeachment cases discussed above. Here we must also emphasize the inherent instability of Romanian politics: apart from competition between opposing political camps, individual parties have experienced bitter internal disputes, parties have split, new ones have been formed, and both electoral and legislative coalitions have changed shape many times since the early 1990s.

Hence the party-political landscape can fluctuate significantly during the five-year term of the president, as particularly Băsescu discovered, and this impacts directly on the influence of the president.

Nor should we exaggerate the powers of the president in government formation (Anghel 2018b; Perju 2015). The preceding analysis clearly illustrates the influence of the president in choosing loyal or friendly prime ministers. Yet this should be not interpreted as a dictatorial position, as the president must always consult the parties, including his own party. According to Article 103(1) of the constitution, the president "shall designate a candidate to the office of Prime Minister, as a result of his consultation with the party which has obtained absolute majority in Parliament, or—unless such majority exists—with the parties represented in Parliament", after which the prime minister designates and the government must receive the support of the parliament. Under cohabitation, the presidents have been forced to nominate prime ministers from competing parties. The same applies to government termination. In line with Article 107(2) of the constitution, Romanian presidents cannot fire prime ministers, although Iliescu, Constantinescu, and Băsescu have each managed to force premiers to resign. Under cohabitation, the position of the prime minister is much safer from presidential pressure. As a result, in both government formation and resignation, the influence of the president depends on the bargaining power of the president's party and on the position of the president within his party.

Otherwise the Romanian case is to a considerable extent in line with our findings from Lithuania. As the preceding analysis confirms, Romanian presidents have interfered in government formation, utilized various channels to influence government decision-making, from ties to political parties and civil society stakeholders to the 'going public' strategy, including via the speeches in the legislature. As in Lithuania, it is therefore appropriate for the Romanian presidents to become actively involved in issues falling under the jurisdiction of the cabinet. And as in Lithuania, such presidential activism is facilitated by low trust in political parties and party politicians and the overall personality-centered political culture. Whether such presidential activism is beneficial for the country can be debated (and is an issue that we shall return to in the concluding chapter), but one can argue that the serious challenges continuing to face Romanian politics provide legitimate grounds for presidential interventions. Interestingly, the Constitutional Court formulated this idea in a non-equivocal manner in its opinion from 2007:

the constitutional prerogatives, as well as the democratic legitimacy granted to the President of Romania by the very way in which he is elected, impose him an active role. The functions of oversight and guarantor granted to the President by Article 80 of the Constitution mean that, by definition, he should attentively observe the existence and operation of the State, vigilantly monitor the modus operandi of public life actors—public authorities, bodies legitimated by the Constitution, civil society—and constantly respect principles and regulations set by the Constitution, as well as defend values established by the fundamental law. The functions of oversight and guarantor cannot be fulfilled in a passive manner, in a state of contemplation, but only by an active and live engagement.[20]

5.4   Concluding Discussion: 'where is it forbidden?'

The behavioral patterns reported in this chapter are in line with our theoretical expectations. Finland has substantially more regular coordination between the two leaders, particularly in the form of bilateral exchanges and through the Ministerial Committee on Foreign and Security Policy, and hence it is not surprising to find that the Finnish president is significantly more constrained than her Lithuanian or Romanian counterparts. It is equally clear that the deliberate and consensual process of constitutional reform in the 1990s contributes to the role of the president. Under the old constitution, and notably during the long reign of President Urho Kekkonen, it was customary for the president to intervene in domestic matters and in the work of the government from its formation to termination. Against the backdrop of such presidential activism, a broad understanding emerged around the need to constrain the presidency so that the government and the Eduskunta would be responsible for domestic and EU affairs while presidential influence would be limited to the field of foreign and security policy. The public seems to favor a stronger presidency, but by and large it is not considered appropriate for the Finnish president to become involved in matters falling under the jurisdiction of the government.

Nonetheless, also in Finland, the constitution leaves room for interpretation. Both presidents Halonen and Niinistö were experienced party politicians with ministerial experience before elected into office, but both have fought hard to safeguard and even expand presidential powers (or at least influence), and there is of course no guarantee that future presidents are equally willing to respect the letter and the spirit of the constitution. In

Lithuania and Romania, on the other hand, several office-holders have possessed much less experience of party politics or have otherwise been less connected to the existing domestic and economic power elites. Such individuals, particularly Presidents Adamkus and Grybauskaité in Lithuania, are more likely to use rhetoric criticizing political parties and their leaders. In both Romania and Lithuania presidents routinely attack the prime minister and the government in their public speeches and interviews, including even in official addresses delivered in the parliament. Here the presidents, as guardians of national interest above the 'dirty deals and shady bargaining' of party politics, benefit from the low trust in parties and political institutions. But interestingly, particularly in Romania, the incumbent presidents remain very much 'party animals', working with and through their political parties. Overall, given the low number of presidents analyzed, it is difficult to draw definitive conclusions about how cohabitation impacts on our findings. Cohabitation reduces presidential influence and makes it substantially more challenging for the president to use informal party channels, but at the same time it seems to contribute to the presidents making active use of other avenues such as public speeches.

In Lithuania and Romania it is considered legitimate for the president to become involved in domestic matters. Apart from legislative vetoes and public speeches, the presidents use a variety of informal channels: active links with the government, the MPs, civil society stakeholders, and also the general public. Unlike in Finland where the size of the presidential office is very small, the Lithuanian and particularly the Romanian presidents have generous staff resources at their disposal. Importantly, their staff are employed primarily to follow developments in policy areas belonging to the competence of the government. To be sure, such presidential activism has also been criticized quite a lot, notably by academics and those politicians in favor of strengthening parliamentarism, but in the personality-centered political cultures found in Central and Eastern European countries, strong and determined leaders are often more popular than constructive 'statesmen'.

The preceding analysis thus confirms that absent of written rules or otherwise strong norms guiding intra-executive coordination, presidents enjoy more discretion in designing their own modes of operation (Lithuania and Romania)—and vice versa (Finland). In line with institutional theory, the adopted approach has become the appropriate course of action, with each new Lithuanian and Romanian president bringing her own staff, personality, and leadership style to the equation. The presidents also enjoy the power of initiative regarding cooperation, and the lack of institutionalized coordination mechanisms can of course facilitate presidential influence. For example, while regular joint meetings might facilitate better coordination, presidents do not necessarily need such bodies. As one Lithuanian interviewee put it: "Presidents that have enough powers do not create such councils, they do not need such kind of institutions, they just arrange ad hoc meetings despite the fact that it is not foreseen in any law." As our analysis indicated, the obvious challenge stemming from lack of rules and a clear understanding of the respective duties of the president and the government is that power can be very much 'up for grabs', particularly when the government is weak or loyal to the president and given the political culture which favors strong leadership and presidential activism. To quote one of our interviewed persons: "one side might ask 'where is it written?' and another can argue 'where is it forbidden?'" Such 'power grabs' apply even to foreign and security policy and EU affairs, themes that we shall explore in the next chapter.

Notes

1. Maria Gestrin-Hagner and Sylvia Bjon, Regeringsordförandena i krismöte—presidenten kritisk till Sannfinländarnas regimskifte, *Hufvudstadsbladet*, 11 June 2017, https://www.hbl.fi/artikel/sauli-niinisto-kritisk-till-regimskiftet-i-sannfinlandarna-regeringskrisen-over-skuggar-gullrandadi/

2. President Sauli Niinistö reveals differences with Prime Minister Sipilä over dissolving government, *Yle*, 13 July 2017, https://yle.fi/uutiset/osasto/news/president_sauli_niinisto_reveals_differences_with_primeminister_sipila_over_dissolving_govt/9721085

3. Information on the president's speeches, press releases, and other activities is available at the website of the presidential office (http://www.tpk.fi).

4. Politiikan suunnitteluun ei tarvita uutta, presidenttivetoista raidetta, *Helsingin Sanomat*, 10 February 2018.

5. When the possibility of government resignation surfaced in June 2018, President Niinistö commented that dissolution of the Sipilä cabinet would not automatically result in early elections. Niinistö said that he would first hear the views of the Eduskunta parties to find out whether it would be possible to form a new government. Marko Junkkari, Presidentti Sauli Niinistö: Hallituksen mahdollinen eronpyyntö ei välttämättä tarkoittaisi uusia vaaleja, *Helsingin Sanomat*, 6 June 2018.

6. According to Meres-Wuori (2014: 225), the two sides have held joint meetings since 1969. While President Halonen met both the Foreign Affairs and Defence Committees, the Foreign Affairs Committee complained on several occasions that it is kept in the dark about the president's activities in external relations. See, for example, Pertti Salolainen, Tieto ulkopolitiikasta ei kulje eduskuntaan, *Helsingin Sanomat*, 18 January 2010.

7. Laki tasavallan presidentin kansliasta 100/2012, http://www.finlex.fi/fi/laki/alkup/2012/20120100

8. The affair concerned leaked emails between Grybauskaité and Eligijus Masiulis, the former leader of the Liberal Movement who had been implicated in a political corruption investigation. Published correspondence dated from 2014 to 2016 and discussed a variety of politically sensitive issues such as court nominations, the 2016 parliamentary elections and who the president would like to be chosen as the prime minister, and warnings about Skvernelis' political ambitions and the president's description of him as a 'dangerous populist' (Park 2018b).

9. Following the first presidential elections in 1993 the cabinet of Bronislovas Lubys resigned in order to enable the president to form the new government. However, the Constitutional Court ruled in early 1998 that the government resigns only upon elections to the Seimas. See "The ruling of the Constitutional Court of the Republic of Lithuania of 10 January 1998, On the programme of the Government of the Republic of Lithuania", http://www.lrkt.lt/en/court-acts/search/170/ta1119/summary

10. Having been forced to appoint the new Social Democratic-led coalition that included the Labour Party, Grybauskaité expressed her frustration through refusing to attend the opening of the Seimas, sending instead her written greetings. There were also accusations of electoral fraud by the Labour Party and Grybauskaité asked the Constitutional Court to investigate the matter.

11. Commenting on Grybauskaité after the first round of the 2014 presidential elections, Kestutis Girnius, a political scientist at the Vilnius Institute of International Relations and Political Science, remarked that "people in Lithuania like her style, the outwardly projected toughness, resoluteness, her willingness to subject any minister to a talk-down". Andrius Sytas, Lithuanian president faces second round in elections, *Reuters*, 12 May 2014, https://www.reuters.com/article/us-lithuania-election/lithuanian-president-faces-second-round-in-elections-idUSBREA4B00920140512

12. Information on the president's speeches, press releases, and other activities is available at the website of the president (http://www.lrp.lt/lt).

13. The document is available in English at https://www.antena3.ro/en/politics/there-is-the-text-of-the-cooperation-agreement-between-president-basescu-and-prime-minister-ponta-196712.html
14. Interestingly, the document also outlined the primary decision-making mechanism for solving conflicts: "The decision making formula between the two components of the Executive, the Presidency and the Romanian Government resides primarily in the meeting or the direct discussion President_Premier. Exceptionally, other persons could be involved, with the prior acceptance of the two, or a topic could be delegated to the administrative system of the two institutions—advisers, technical staff."
15. Carmen Paun, Romanian president calls on prime minister to resign, *Politico*, 27 April 2018, https://www.politico.eu/article/klaus-iohannis-viorica-dancila-romania-president-calls-on-prime-minister-to-resign/
16. Andrew Rettman, Romanian leaders trade jibes over upcoming EU presidency, *EUobserver*, 12 November 2018, https://euobserver.com/institutional/143357
17. http://www.presidency.ro/en/commitments/president-klaus-iohannis-country-project
18. Information on the president's speeches and other activities is available at http://www.presidency.ro/en
19. The Constitutional Court has also ruled that it is legal for the president to maintain such ties to parties: "the Constitution does not forbid the President to maintain his relationships with the political party that provided him support throughout the elections or with any other political parties. Such a ban would not be in the spirit of the Constitution if the President is elected based on a direct, individual vote, owing to his political agenda and if he is accountable to his constituencies for the fulfillment of this program. It is obvious that in order to put in practice his program, the President may carry out a dialogue with the political party whose member he used to be or with a completely different political party that could provide support in terms of the implementation of this program." Advisory Opinion no. 1/2007, published in the Official Journal no. 258/18 April 2007 (Tănăsescu 2008). Two other court decisions also deal with this issue. Decision no. 53/2005 and Decision no. 284/2014 stated that "the President's right to express political opinions arguing in accordance with his political program or to militate in order to materialize these opinions is not contrary to the constitutional interdiction regarding the membership of a political party" (Gherghina et al. 2016: 5).
20. Advisory Opinion no. 1/2007, published in the Official Journal no. 258/18 April 2007.

BIBLIOGRAPHY

Adamkus, V. (2004). *Be nutylėjimų: dienoraščiai, vertinimai, pastabos paraštėse.* Vilnius: Tyto alba.

Anghel, V. (2017). Alliance-Building Strategies in Post-Communist Romania (1990–2016): Bonding Through Dependence? *Südosteuropa Mitteilungen, 57*(3), 16–29.

Anghel, V. (2018a, February 19). Romania – An Underused Presidency? *Presidential Power* blog. http://presidential-power.com/?p=7681

Anghel, V. (2018b). "Why Can't We Be Friends?" The Coalition Potential of Presidents in Semi-Presidential Republics—Insights from Romania. *East European Politics and Societies and Cultures, 32*(1), 101–118.

Brazauskas, A. (2007). *Ir Tuomet Dirbome Lietuvai: Faktai, Atsiminimai, Komentarai.* Vilnius: Knygiai.

Bucur, C. (2016, March 16). Romania – President Iohannis' Contested Performance and a Brief Assessment of His Exercise of Constitutional Powers. *Presidential Power* blog. http://presidential-power.com/?p=4614

Bucur, C. (2017, January 12). Romania – The Politics of the Fourth Cohabitation. *Presidential Power* blog. http://presidential-power.com/?p=5848

Elgie, R. (2018). *Political Leadership: A Pragmatic Institutionalist Approach.* London: Palgrave Macmillan.

Gallagher, T., & Andrievici, V. (2008). Romania: Political Irresponsibility Without Constitutional Safeguards. In R. Elgie & S. Moestrup (Eds.), *Semi-Presidentialism in Central and Eastern Europe* (pp. 138–158). Manchester: Manchester University Press.

Gherghina, S. (2013). Formal and Informal Powers in a Semi-Presidential Regime: The Case of Romania. In V. Hloušek et al. (Eds.), *Presidents Above Parties? Presidents in Central and Eastern Europe, Their Formal Competencies and Informal Power* (pp. 257–270). Brno: Masaryk University.

Gherghina, S., & Hein, M. (2016). Romania. In A. Fruhstorfer & M. Hein (Eds.), *Constitutional Politics in Central and Eastern Europe: From Post-Socialist Transition to the Reform of Political Systems* (pp. 173–197). Wiesbaden: Springer.

Gherghina, S., & Miscoiu, S. (2013). The Failure of Cohabitation: Explaining the 2007 and 2012 Institutional Crises in Romania. *East European Politics & Societies and Cultures, 27*(4), 668–684.

Gherghina, S., Iancu, A., & Soare, S. (2016, September). *Presidents and Their Parties: Insights from Romania.* Paper presented at the ECPR General Conference, Prague.

Guțan, M. (2012). Romanian Semi-Presidentialism in Historical Context. *Romanian Journal of Comparative Law, 2*, 275–303.

Hallberg, P., Martikainen, T., Nousiainen, J., & Tiikkainen, P. (2009). *Presidentin valta: hallitsijanvallan ja parlamentarismin välinen jännite Suomessa 1919–2009.* Helsinki: WSOY.

Hämäläinen, U. (2013). Niinistö mukautui yhteisjohtajaksi. In S. Tiihonen, M. Pohls, & J. Korppi-Tommola (Eds.), *Presidentti johtaa: Suomalaisen valtiojohtamisen pitkä linja* (pp. 279–300). Helsinki: Siltala.

Iusmen, I. (2015). EU Leverage and Democratic Backsliding in Central and Eastern Europe: The Case of Romania. *Journal of Common Market Studies, 53*(3), 593–608.

Karvonen, L. (2016). No Definite Decline. The Power of Political Parties in Finland: A Focused Analysis. In L. Karvonen, H. Paloheimo, & T. Raunio (Eds.), *The Changing Balance of Political Power in Finland* (pp. 91–125). Stockholm: Santérus Academic Press.

Köker, P. (2014a, January 13). Lithuania – President Grybauskaite's Veto Activity. *Presidential Power* blog. https://presidential-power.com/?p=575

Köker, P. (2014b, July 17). Lithuania – Reshuffle of Deputy Ministers as President Grybauskaite Is Sworn in for Second Term in Office. *Presidential Power* blog. http://presidential-power.com/?p=1648

Köker, P. (2017). *Presidential Activism and Veto Power in Central and Eastern Europe.* Cham: Palgrave Macmillan.

Krupavičius, A. (2008). Semi-Presidentialism in Lithuania: Origins, Development and Challenges. In R. Elgie & S. Moestrup (Eds.), *Semi-Presidentialism in Central and Eastern Europe* (pp. 65–84). Manchester: Manchester University Press.

Krupavičius, A. (2013). Lithuania's President: A Formal and Informal Power. In V. Hloušek et al. (Eds.), *Presidents Above Parties? Presidents in Central and Eastern Europe, Their Formal Competencies and Informal Power* (pp. 205–232). Brno: Masaryk University.

Levai, M. C., & Tomescu, C. (2012). Atribuțiile Președintelui României în raport cu Parlamentul – aspecte teoretice și practice. *Revista Transilvană de Științe Administrative, 30*(1), 84–105.

Matsuzato, K., & Gudžinskas, L. (2006). An Eternally Unfinished Parliamentary Regime? Semipresidentialism as a Prism to View Lithuanian Politics. *Acta Slavica Iaponica, 23,* 146–170.

Meres-Wuori, O. (2014). *Valta ja valtiosääntö, Suomen ulko- ja turvallisuuspoliittinen valtajärjestelmä.* Helsinki: Unigrafia.

Mörttinen, M., & Nurmi, L. (2018). *Sauli Niinistö: Mäntyniemen herra.* Helsinki: Into.

Nakrošis, V., Vilpišauskas, R., & Barcevičius, E. (2018). Making Change Happen: Policy Dynamics in the Adoption of Major Reforms in Lithuania. *Public Policy and Administration,* First view. https://doi.org/10.1177/09520767 18755568.

Norkus, Z. (2013). Parliamentarism Versus Semi-Presidentialism in the Baltic States: The Causes and Consequences of Differences in the Constitutional Framework. *Baltic Journal of Political Science, 2,* 7–28.

Park, A. (2018a, October 11). Lithuania – President Grybauskaite in a Continuous Intra-institutional Tug of War (Part 2). *Presidential Power* blog. http://presidential-power.com/?p=8754

Park, A. (2018b, July 11). Lithuania – President Grybauskaite in an Intra-institutional Tug of War. *Presidential Power* blog. http://presidential-power.com/?p=8427

Perju, V. (2015). The Romanian Double Executive and the 2012 Constitutional Crisis. *International Journal of Constitutional Law, 13*(1), 246–278.

Sedelius, T. (2006). *The Tug-of-War between Presidents and Prime Ministers: Semi-Presidentialism in Central and Eastern Europe.* Örebro: Örebro Studies in Political Science 15.

Tănăsescu, E. S. (2008). The President of Romania or the Slippery Slope of a Political Regime. *European Constitutional Law Review, 4*(1), 64–97.

Tiilikainen, T. (2013). Tarja Halonen – presidentti puolustuskannalla. In S. Tiihonen, M. Pohls, & J. Korppi-Tommola (Eds.), *Presidentti johtaa: Suomalaisen valtiojohtamisen pitkä linja* (pp. 258–277). Helsinki: Siltala.

Urbanavičius, D. (1999). Lithuania. In R. Elgie (Ed.), *Semi-Presidentialism in Europe* (pp. 150–169). Oxford: Oxford University Press.

Verheijen, T. (1999). Romania. In R. Elgie (Ed.), *Semi-Presidentialism in Europe* (pp. 193–215). Oxford: Oxford University Press.

Yli-Huttula, T. (2018). *Presidentti ja porvarivalta: Ristiriitoja ja yhteistoimintaa tasavallan sisäpiirissä.* Helsinki: Otava.

CHAPTER 6

Decision-Making in Foreign and Security Policies and EU Affairs

Whereas the two previous chapters have analyzed overall intra-executive coordination, the final empirical chapter zooms in on foreign and security policy and EU affairs, examining decision-making and division of labor between the president and the prime minister. We again highlight the role of institutions, but also show how constitutional rules about jurisdictions bend in favor of presidents. This applies particularly to the question of who represents the country in the European Council, an issue that has proven particularly controversial in all three countries. We also pay special attention to defense policy, another policy domain where power is shared between the two executives.

Constitutionally the three countries are broadly similar when it comes to external relations. The president either leads (Lithuania and Romania) or co-leads (Finland) foreign and security policy and is the Commander-in-Chief of the Armed Forces, but Finland stands out on account of having the prime minister represent the country at the European-level top summits. The chapter is again divided into three country sections and a concluding summary. In line with our theoretical argument about external relations and particularly security policy forming a 'special case', we expect to find more coordination in foreign and security policy than in domestic matters. We should also see behavioral norms that underline the importance of the country speaking with one voice in international politics.

© The Author(s) 2020
T. Raunio, T. Sedelius, *Semi-Presidential Policy-Making in Europe*,
Palgrave Studies in Presidential Politics,
https://doi.org/10.1007/978-3-030-16431-7_6

127

6.1   FINLAND: ESTABLISHING A LOGICAL DIVISION
OF LABOR

Finland certainly belongs to those countries where national unity is emphasized in security policy. During the Cold War foreign policy was very much driven by the concept of neutrality: political debate and contestation on security policy were rare and maintaining amicable relations with the Soviet Union was a top priority. When the Soviet Union collapsed, Finland wasted no time becoming fully engaged in European integration, joining the EU in 1995.

The fall of the Soviet bloc and EU membership also acted as catalysts for constitutional change from the early 1990s onward. Under the old constitutional regime foreign policy was the exclusive domain of the president, and hence the new constitution, which entered into force in 2000, has for the first time granted the Eduskunta genuine authority in external affairs. The government is responsible for EU policy, with foreign policy leadership shared between the president and the government. According to Section 93 of the new constitution:

> The foreign policy of Finland is directed by the President of the Republic in co-operation with the Government. However, the Parliament accepts Finland's international obligations and their denouncement and decides on the bringing into force of Finland's international obligations in so far as provided in this Constitution. The President decides on matters of war and peace, with the consent of the Parliament.
>
> The Government is responsible for the national preparation of the decisions to be made in the European Union, and decides on the concomitant Finnish measures, unless the decision requires the approval of the Parliament. The Parliament participates in the national preparation of decisions to be made in the European Union, as provided in this Constitution.
>
> The communication of important foreign policy positions to foreign States and international organizations is the responsibility of the Minister with competence in foreign affairs.

European policy belongs almost exclusively to the jurisdiction of the government. The government decides Finland's positions and represents the country in the Council and the European Council. The jurisdiction of the government covers all EU matters, but in CFSP/CSDP the government must act in 'close cooperation' with the president. The president is thus not part of the routine national EU coordination system, but is consulted in foreign and security policy issues. Regarding Treaty changes negotiated in Intergovernmental Conferences (IGC), the prime minister's office is responsible for the preparations and the prime minister represents Finland in the bargaining, but at least until now the president has decided on the ratification of the Treaty in a presidential session of the government (Hyvärinen and Raunio 2014).

The Foreign Affairs Committee (FAC) of the Eduskunta considers EU issues pertaining to foreign and security policy, while according to Section 97 of the constitution, it "shall receive from the Government, upon request and when otherwise necessary, reports of matters pertaining to foreign and security policy". Finally, the Eduskunta must approve all international obligations and commitments with legislative or budgetary implications. This empowerment of the Eduskunta in foreign and security policy enjoyed broad support among political parties. Research indicates that the Eduskunta also uses actively its new-won powers, with the Foreign Affairs Committee not only insisting on government fulfilling its reporting obligations but also requesting further information from the cabinet. Ex ante mechanisms are crucial, with the FAC receiving information from the government and hearing ministers ahead of EU or international meetings (Raunio 2016, 2018). And as explained in Chap. 5, during the presidency of Niinistö, contacts between the president and the Eduskunta and particularly its Foreign Affairs Committee have intensified considerably, meaning that MPs receive more information about the views and actions of the president in foreign affairs questions. Niinistö also meets regularly, twice a year, the chairs of all the Eduskunta party groups, and these meetings can also be seen as a way to build national consensus in foreign and security policy. The meetings with Eduskunta committees and party group leaders are always held behind closed doors, with a strict code of confidentiality observed by all participants.

The Constitutional Law Committee of the Eduskunta stipulated before the constitution entered into force the following rules for foreign policy formulation and decision-making:

> The president must make all significant foreign policy decisions and actions together with the government and on the basis of the government's preparatory work. The actual forms of cooperation will depend on the significance of the issues. In broad-ranging matters discussions between president and the entire government are required. In more urgent matters it may, however, be sufficient for the president to consult the [Ministerial] Committee on Foreign and Security Policy or an individual minister, primarily the prime minister, foreign minister, or the minister responsible for preparing the issue.[1]

As already explained in Chap. 4, in practice co-leadership is executed through the Ministerial Committee on Foreign and Security Policy and essentially weekly dialogue between the president and the prime minister and the foreign minister. The work of the ministerial committee is strictly confidential and its decisions are taken by consensus. The same applies to bilateral exchanges between the leaders, with the notion of 'speaking with one voice' very much emphasized in the domestic foreign and security policy discourse (Oikeusministeriö 2002; Tiilikainen 2003; Raunio 2008, 2012). Particularly the bilateral meetings facilitate more in-depth discussions and exchange of views. By and large co-leadership has functioned smoothly, although there have been differences of opinion between the president and the government or some individual ministers, with both Presidents Halonen and particularly Niinistö occasionally publicly questioning or criticizing the comments made by ministers. Also quite rarely has the president, the government, or the Eduskunta complained that information did not arrive in timely fashion.

In terms of strategic planning and the broad lines of national foreign and security policy, a key role is performed by the 'grand strategy document', the Government Security and Defence Policy Report that is published roughly every four years. The government drafts the report, the parliament monitors the process, and the president is kept up to date, not least through the Ministerial Committee on Foreign and Security Policy. The president's office can be represented in the working group preparing the report. Otherwise defense policy—including questions related to national defense forces—is handled by the government and the Ministry of Defence that are accountable to the Eduskunta and to its defence committee. However, the president is actively consulted in such matters and again there is regular dialogue between the president and the government at various levels. The Ministerial Committee on Foreign and Security Policy can be seen as a kind of national security council that one finds in Lithuania and Romania, as its agenda covers also matters dealing with national defense and strategic planning. Bilateral exchanges between the president and the prime minister and the foreign minister can of course also be used for discussing security and defense policy if needed.

Without any doubt the biggest challenge has been drawing a clear line between EU affairs and foreign policy matters. The strong links between EU decisions and particularly the development of CFSP/CSDP and other national foreign policy questions make such categorizations inherently difficult, as European-level coordination processes and policy choices increasingly influence national foreign and security policies. While the effectiveness of CFSP/CSDP can be questioned, it is plausible to argue that the linkage between the two levels—national foreign policies and EU's external relations—will become even stronger in the future.[2] Hence it is completely logical that the presidents have tried to legitimize their role in EU affairs and particularly CFSP/CSDP matters through the strong linkage between European and foreign policies—a finding that applies also to Lithuania and Romania. In order for the president to genuinely lead foreign policy, the president must also be actively involved in EU policy. To quote President Halonen: "It is not possible to discuss foreign and security policy without considering the influence of the Union. EU penetrates everything."[3] This in turn can result in intra-executive jurisdictional disputes.

Perhaps the best example is from autumn 2005 when the government introduced the Act on Military Crisis Management and certain associated Acts (HE 110/2005). According to the proposed law, the president—as the Commander-in-Chief of the Armed Forces (Section 128 of the constitution)—would have decided on Finland's participation in EU-led crisis management operations. However, the Constitutional Law Committee disagreed, stating that the government should take the decision regarding both the participation and the deployment of national units for the operations. The committee emphasized the strong interdependence between the preparatory work carried out in the EU institutions and the national decision on participation. It would be illogical if the government was responsible for the earlier stages of the policy process and the president for the decision on whether to participate, as the latter is obviously influenced by the former. But the committee was not unanimous, and importantly, the majority of the experts heard by the committee—mainly professors of law with long-standing expertise in constitutional questions—saw that the president should decide on Finland's participation (Niskanen 2006, 2009: 141–145). As a result, the president takes the final decisions about sending troops abroad. However, the government remains the key actor, negotiating about operations abroad and planning Finnish participation, and the president—who is naturally consulted throughout the decision-making processes—has not contested the decisions.

Another good example is relations with Russia—always a salient issue for Finland. Constitutionally bilateral relations with foreign states fall under the co-leadership of Section 93, but Finnish-Russian relations are increasingly influenced by the EU, not least because trade policy is in the competence of the Union. During the presidency of Halonen the president and the prime minister had several behind-the-scenes disputes about who is the leading actor toward Russia. Furthermore, when Finland held the EU presidency in the latter half of 2006, there were disagreements between the government and the president about who should chair some of the meetings between EU and third countries. The prime minister emerged victorious, as it was interpreted that during the EU presidency the Finnish representative was in the meetings primarily representing the Union, not Finland. Following the Lisbon Treaty the government appoints delegations to summits between the EU and third countries.[4] President Niinistö in turn has maintained regular bilateral contacts with the Russian president, showing particular activism following Russian invasion of Ukraine in 2014.[5]

But the problem that really symbolized these jurisdictional conflicts was the policy of 'two plates'—dual representation in the European Council. The Constitutional Law Committee decided prior to EU membership that the prime minister should represent Finland in the European Council. However, according to President Martti Ahtisaari (1994–2000), the president should have the right to decide on his participation in the European Council. In May 1995 Prime Minister Paavo Lipponen announced a statement, formulated jointly with the president's office, according to which the prime minister will always attend the European Council and the president as she chooses. The Eduskunta and its Constitutional Law Committee subsequently readopted their position several times, arguing that this would facilitate parliamentary control and would also be logical as the government's competence covers all EU matters. In significant CFSP/CSDP matters and on issues relating to the foreign policies of the member states on the agenda of the European Council, the government should act in close cooperation with the president.

Until the Lisbon Treaty entered into force, President Halonen participated in the majority of European Council meetings (Niskanen 2009: 175–186). When the president attended the European Council, the foreign minister had to leave the meeting room—despite the fact that agenda items had been prepared by the prime minister's office (perhaps together with the foreign ministry) and belonged to the competence of the government. The question was very important in terms of parliamentary accountability. The prime minister must inform both beforehand and afterward the Grand Committee, the EU committee of the Eduskunta, of European

Council meetings, with the Foreign Affairs Committee enjoying similar rights in CFSP matters. Moreover, dual representation arguably made it more difficult for foreign observers to understand who leads Finnish EU policy. It is probable that not all of the politicians in the European Council, or the media covering the meetings, knew the wording of the Finnish constitution.

The Lisbon Treaty formalized the position of the European Council as one of the EU institutions, and this provided an 'external' solution to the policy of two plates. After the Lisbon Treaty entered into force, each country is represented in the European Council by either its prime minister or the head of state. The government and the Eduskunta agreed that the prime minister would be representing Finland. According to the government's bill for amending the constitution, the prime minister would represent Finland in the European Council and in other EU meetings where the political leaders of the member states are represented (such as informal meetings between the leaders of member states and summits between the EU and third countries). However, to the extent that this is possible within the EU framework, the government could in exceptional circumstances decide that also the president represents Finland in EU meetings. The presence of both the prime minister and the president would, so the argument goes, indicate that the issue is of particular salience to Finland and would also strengthen Finland's bargaining position.[6] Hence, according to a constitutional amendment (Section 66) from 2012, "The Prime minister represents Finland on the European Council. Unless the Government exceptionally decides otherwise, the Prime minister also represents Finland in other activities of the European Union requiring the participation of the highest level of State".

The Finnish case has also wider relevance in terms of foreign policy leadership. Essentially the constitutional requirement of co-leadership means that both the president and the government possess the right of veto in foreign policy. Put in another way, all foreign affairs decisions and positions should be agreed upon by both executives. Hence potential deadlocks were feared, and a new clause (Section 58) was added to the constitution in 2012 according to which the position of the Eduskunta is decisive in cases of disagreements between the president and the government. However, only a small share of foreign policy matters, basically those issues necessitating formal decision-making, would be decided under that procedure (Hovila 2014). As result, disagreements between the two executives can continue to produce policy deadlock and will favor the status quo. Moreover, despite regular and active intra-executive coordination, it is in any case practically impossible to keep track of what the prime minister and the president do in foreign policy. Both executives meet foreign leaders and hold speeches both at home and abroad, and can thus further their own objectives, particularly when considering the confidential nature of the meetings with foreign leaders (Niskanen 2009: 249–267; Hallberg et al. 2009: 320–371).[7]

A final point concerns the tricky question of balance of power—which one, the president or the prime minister, actually leads under co-leadership? Indeed, even the first sentence of Section 93 is open to different interpretations, depending on whether one emphasizes the beginning ('directed by the President') or the end ('in cooperation with the Government') of the sentence.[8] On the one hand, the organizational set-up and the constitutional rules tend to favor the government. While contacts between the president's office and particularly the foreign ministry are very active, the Finnish president has hardly any administrative machinery of her own and is thus dependent on the preparatory work carried out by the government (see Chap. 5).[9] This applies particularly to EU matters, CFSP/CSDP included, where also the formal decision-making power and the right to represent Finland at the European level belongs to the government. The prime minister represents Finland in European Council, and this further marginalizes the president as foreign and security policy questions appear essentially on the agenda of every European Council summit.[10]

On the other hand, contextual factors certainly impact on the balance of power. Cohabitation matters, as the role of the president was more limited from 2003 to 2012 when the Social Democratic President Halonen shared power from 2003 onward with center-right prime ministers. During his tenure in office President Niinistö in turn has shared power with cabinets led by center-right prime ministers, and this has clearly contributed to smoother co-leadership in foreign policy and to stronger presidential influence. Already before taking office, Niinistö had been very critical of the plans to further reduce the powers invested in the presidency, especially regarding foreign policy leadership (Hämäläinen 2013; Yli-Huttula 2018: 143–157). In Chap. 4 it was already reported that there is evidence that Niinistö has dominated the proceedings in the Ministerial Committee on Foreign and Security Policy and has been able to carve a prominent position for himself in foreign affairs. Presidential activism has been facilitated by the fact that since the 2015 parliamentary elections, Prime Minister Juha Sipilä, who has background in business, has prioritized domestic issues, such as reviving the economy and the re-organization of social and health services. Furthermore, Niinistö's activism need to be understood in the context of developments in neighboring Russia, whose aggressive foreign policy has created unwelcome tensions in Eastern and Northern Europe. As mentioned earlier, Niinistö has met the Russian President Putin regularly, showing particular activism following Russian invasion of Ukraine in 2014, has visited the White House, has attended various international conferences on security policy, and even hosted a high-profile summit between Presidents Trump and Putin in Helsinki in the summer of 2018. This has ensured high visibility for Niinistö in the domestic media. People appreciate solid leadership in external affairs from the president and by all accounts Niinistö has met such expectations.

6.2   Lithuania: Presidential 'Power Grabs'

In Lithuania and Romania the situation is constitutionally more straightforward than in Finland, as in both countries foreign policy leadership is in the hands of the president. However, in both Lithuania and Romania, the government is also involved in implementing foreign policy, thus creating challenges for coordination. In EU affairs the equation is much more complicated and open for competing jurisdictional interpretations, as neither the Lithuanian nor the Romanian constitution provides any detailed rules about how European matters are handled domestically or about who represents the country in the European Council.

According to Article 84 of the Lithuanian constitution, the president "1) shall decide the basic issues of foreign policy and, together with the Government, conduct foreign policy; [and] 2) shall sign international treaties of the Republic of Lithuania and submit them to the Seimas for ratification". Hence the legislature has the right to ratify various international treaties, including those related to political and economic cooperation, participation in international organizations, and defense policy (Article 138). In addition, the president is the Commander-in-Chief of the Armed Forces and chairs the State Defence Council (Article 140). Regarding the European Union, a special law supplementing the constitution in rather basic terms defines the role of the government and the participation rights of the Seimas and its European Affairs and Foreign Affairs Committees, which are broadly similar, although somewhat less specific than the participation rights of the Finnish Eduskunta and its committees. Significantly, the law remains quiet about representation at the European level.[11]

Starting with security and defense policy, the role of the State Defence Council was already elaborated upon in Chap. 4. Chaired by the president, its members are the prime minister, the defence minister, the speaker of the parliament, and the Commander of the Armed Forces. It is clearly the highest and most important body for coordinating and taking decisions on questions related to Lithuanian security and defense policy. Our interviewees emphasized that the Council has been very firmly under the control of the president, particularly in recent years during the presidency of Grybauskaitė. The president can quite freely decide when the Council convenes and which topics receive attention. In addition, there was a Foreign Policy Coordination Council chaired by the president from 1993 to 2004.[12]

Relations with neighboring Russia are obviously of very high salience for Lithuania. Therefore Russian aggressive foreign policy, and specifically the war in Ukraine and the annexation of Crimea by Russia in 2014, has caused understandable anxiety in Lithuania. These recent developments have also impacted on the balance of power between the two executives. Under normal circumstances, it is the government and particularly the Ministry of Defence together with the Commander of the Armed Forces that are responsible for the administration and command of the armed forces. According to Šlekys (2018) the heightened tensions in the region in 2014 were the first time since the 1990s that Lithuania had to take questions of defense more seriously. Until then the successive ministers of defense enjoyed quite strong autonomy inside the government. More significantly, the presidents had not displayed any real interest in defense policy beyond certain related questions, with for example Grybauskaitė focusing on energy security and the reform of the intelligence services in her first term. Presidents had also been consulted about the selection of foreign and defense ministers. During her first term Grybauskaitė had convened the State Defence Council only five times, with two of these meetings held after the annexation of Crimea in the spring of 2014. But this changed almost overnight after the war in Ukraine started.

In the spring of 2014 the main Lithuanian political parties signed an agreement according to which the national military budget will reach the 2 percent of gross domestic product (GDP) required by NATO in the period from 2014 to 2020. In March 2014 President Grybauskaitė declared publicly that the Labour Party, a member of the ruling coalition cabinet, might be operating under undue influence from Moscow. As a result, Grybauskaitė announced that any representative of the Labour

Party would not be invited to attend the sessions of the State Defence Council. It is probable that Grybauskaitė's behavior was driven by her distrust or dislike of the Labour Party and its leading politicians. However, the problem was that the speaker of the Seimas, Loreta Graužinienė from the Labour Party, had the constitutional right according to Article 140 to participate in the meetings of the State Defence Council. While the issue was solved over the next couple of months, it was a clear sign that Grybauskaitė was intending to become actively involved in defense matters.

Later that spring Grybauskaitė was re-elected (of course Grybauskaitė's sudden interest in defense issues may also have been influenced by the approaching presidential elections), and this provided her with extra vigor to stamp her authority in defense policy. In May 2014 a budgetary dispute emerged, with the Ministry of Defence advocating additional funding for the remainder of the year by around 130 million Litas (roughly 35 million euros), but the Ministry of Finance replied that only a few additional millions could be forthcoming. However, Grybauskaitė stepped in and in one of her first speeches in the second term declared that defense policy would be a priority and that additional money for not just 2014 but also 2015 should be found. In the end the Seimas voted in favor of extra money for defense policy in line with the intervention from the president.

Another intra-executive disagreement surfaced in 2015 over the reintroduction of conscription. Early that year Grybauskaitė summoned the Commander of the Armed Forces to discuss the needs of the armed forces. Soon after the meeting President Grybauskaitė announced her intention of reintroducing conscription, with the announcement catching everyone, including the minister of defense and the Commander of the Armed Forces, by surprise. Then Grybauskaitė convened the State Defence Council for 24 February. In a meeting lasting less than an hour, the Council showed the green light to go ahead with a temporary reinstatement of compulsory military service based on recruiting 3500 conscripts per year. Even though voting in favor of the decision in the State Defence Council, the defense minister, Juozas Olekas from the Social Democratic Party, was very skeptical, including in his public remarks. The media immediately spotted the disagreement between the two executives, or at least between Grybauskaitė and Olekas. However, disagreements continued about what should happen to conscription after 2020. Grybauskaitė, together with some influential figures, not least Artūras Paulauskas, the chair of the Seimas' Committee on National Security and Defence, suggested that conscription should continue indefinitely. Prime Minister

Butkevičius and Olekas wanted to proceed more gradually, but again the position of the president prevailed and in the summer of 2016 the Seimas voted in favor of continuous conscription (Šlekys 2018).

On account of the (successful) presidential intervention in defense budget and the reintroduction of conscription, many commentators drew the conclusion that now defense policy had shifted under the control of the presidential palace. This gave President Grybauskaitė also much media exposure, as in the context of heightened regional tensions and alarm caused by Russian aggressive foreign policy, defense matters climbed to the top of the domestic political agenda. Yet, as pointed earlier, from 2012 until 2016 Grybauskaitė shared power with the coalition led by the Social Democratic Party of Lithuania (LSDP), and this certainly limited her freedom of maneuver in other policy sectors. But when we limit our focus to just security and defense policy, our analysis certainly provides evidence of the president inserting her authority in an issue area previously handled by the government. The developments are also in line with the securitization thesis outlined in our theoretical framework (Chap. 2), whereby President Grybauskaitė—as the leader of the country and head of the armed forces—benefited from an external threat.[13]

Another power grab with arguably more far-reaching consequences deals with representation in the European Council. In Lithuania, the constitution, secondary laws, or the rules about domestic EU coordination do not detail who should represent the country in the European Council. However, European affairs are nonetheless the domain of the government, with the prime minister leading Lithuanian integration policy. The cabinet and particularly the Ministry of Foreign Affairs is thus responsible for coordinating EU matters and for preparatory work ahead of the Council and the European Council, but informal contacts between the government, the Seimas, and the president's office are important, especially in terms of resolving interinstitutional disagreements. According to the legal provisions, the government must consult the president about issues to be debated in the European Council as well as on issues related to national foreign and security policy. The Foreign Affairs Committee and the European Affairs Committee of the Seimas issue opinions to the president before the European Council meetings. The Foreign Affairs Committee can also ask for an opinion from the president, which is then usually presented by her advisers. While the Seimas receives ex post information about decisions taken in the European Council, the president does not have to report to or appear in the parliament after the summits (Gärtner et al. 2011; Vilpišauskas 2015).

President Adamkus participated in those European Council meetings or covered those agenda points that featured foreign and security policy while the prime minister covered other matters. Often both executives would attend the summits. Adamkus displayed keen interest in certain EU questions, notably EU's Eastern Neighbourhood Policy, energy policy, as well as preparations for adopting the euro, but in general leadership in EU matters belonged to the government. President Grybauskaitė in turn has participated in the European Council, even though constitutional provisions about division of labor at least suggest that the prime minister should represent Lithuania. Overall, the influence of Grybauskaitė has certainly been quite strong in EU affairs, including in the economic sphere, partly because Grybauskaitė had served previously as the finance minister and as the EU Commissioner for Financial Programming and the Budget. The prime ministers regardless of their party-political affiliation have not contested this arrangement, not least because of Grybauskaitė's popularity. According to one interviewee, "the leader which enjoys public support can easily do such things ad hoc, therefore it was possible to establish certain practices without any legal documents—just like with attendance of the meetings of the European Council". The lack of contestation was also aided by the weakness of the government, as Prime Minister Kubilius needed presidential support for the austerity measures. Here it must be emphasized that the Lisbon Treaty, following which either the prime minister or the president represents the member state in the European Council, entered into force just at the time when the Kubilius cabinet was suffering from the economic crisis. Grybauskaitė was also highly prominent during Lithuania's EU presidency in the latter half of 2013 and intervened more than President Adamkus in the formulation of national negotiating positions.[14] Nonetheless, even during Grybauskaitė's presidency, it is the government that is responsible for the routine handling and domestic coordination of EU issues, with sectoral ministers representing Lithuania in the Council of Ministers. Hence the president attends the European Council, but the government remains arguably more influential in Lithuanian-EU relations (Maniokas and Vilpišauskas 2010; Krupavičius 2013: 215; Vilpišauskas 2015).

Of the Lithuanian presidents, Grybauskaitė has been particularly determined to maintain full command of foreign and security policy. A good illustration of her position came in the form of frustration expressed by Prime Minister Skvernelis about leadership in Lithuanian foreign policy. Skvernelis had on several occasions voiced his concerns about presidential dominance in both foreign and EU affairs and how there was room for improvement in intra-executive coordination. For instance, in December

2017 Skvernelis commented in an interview that there had been no communication with the government about a vote in the United Nations, where Lithuania had unexpectedly voted in favor of the resolution that condemned the United States' formal recognition of Jerusalem as the capital of Israel. In early 2018 Prime Minister Skvernelis announced in a radio interview his intention of reviving an intergovernmental commission between Lithuania and Russia. The prime minister argued that such a commission would be beneficial for Lithuania's national economic and security interests and would open a dialogue with Russia. The initiative of Skvernelis clearly broke with the official foreign policy line of Grybauskaitė, who subsequently issued a statement outlining, "when Russia will change its aggressive policy towards the [neighboring] states, when it returns occupied territories, and when it cedes violating international law by meddling into other countries' elections, then we will be ready to start a closer cooperation". More importantly from our point of view, Grybauskaitė sent a strong signal to Skvernelis that "his initiatives were not welcomed, that such proposals were irresponsible from the national security standpoint, and that as a head of state in charge of foreign policy she had no intention of changing the status quo that Lithuania finds itself in with Russia" (Park 2018b). In April 2018 Skvernelis invited the foreign minister and several Lithuanian ambassadors for discussions about Lithuanian relations with Russia, Ukraine, Georgia, and Moldova. Again Grybauskaitė was not amused, pointing out that foreign policy was her sphere of influence (Park 2018a).

In the preceding analysis we have deliberately mainly focused on two key policy areas or questions—security and defense policy and representation in the European Council—as they are very informative in terms of our theoretical framework. In the absence of clear formal rules and coordination mechanisms, the rules can be bent, and in both cases from Lithuania they have bent in favor of the president. Our analysis and the overview of formal coordination instruments in Chap. 4 also show that intra-executive coordination is most established in foreign and security policy. For the most part foreign policy leadership has functioned without any major problems, and here of course one must remember that foreign policy is led by the president, with the government constitutionally only involved in the implementation of the policy.[15] In that capacity, the prime minister also meets foreign leaders and communicates Lithuanian's positions in foreign policy questions, but leadership is in the hands of the president. Hence intra-executive jurisdictional disputes are less likely to emerge than in Finland. Key foreign policy choices, such as those concerning EU and NATO memberships, were coordinated between all three key state institutions—the president, the government, and the Seimas. Meetings with foreign leaders or visits abroad are closely coordinated, with the Ministry of Foreign Affairs performing a key role.

6.3   Romania: President as the Undisputed Leader in Foreign Affairs

The Romanian constitution, inspired by the French experience, states very clearly that "the President of Romania shall represent the Romanian State and is the safeguard of the national independence, unity and territorial integrity of the country" (Article 80(1)). Article 91(1) stipulates, "the President shall, in the name of Romania, conclude international treaties negotiated by the Government, and then submit them to the Parliament for ratification". The president is also the Commander-in-Chief of the Armed Forces and presides over the Supreme Council of National Defence (Article 92). The government, in turn, shall "ensure the implementation of the domestic and foreign policy of the country, and exercise the general management of public administration" (Article 102(1)). The constitution says nothing about the domestic coordination of EU matters or who represents Romania at the European level.

Hence in line with the French model presidential leadership in external relations has never been seriously questioned, not even during periods of cohabitation. To be sure, the government and particularly the foreign ministry are actively involved in the implementation of both foreign and European policy. For example, as in Lithuania, membership negotiations with both the EU and the NATO were primarily carried out by the government, and key foreign policy choices have been coordinated between the president, the cabinet, and the legislature, not least because the approval of the parliament is required for international treaties. This division of labor was also recognized in the 'cohabitation pact' agreed between Prime Minister Ponta and President Băsescu following the 2012 impeachment crisis and the parliamentary elections (see Chap. 5). According to the pact the president was to be responsible for foreign affairs, with the government in charge of domestic economic and social matters. The cohabitation pact also specifically outlined that in order not to create disputes regarding Romania's commitment to international and European institutions, "there are effective areas where cooperation between the two parties of the executive is required". These included "elaboration of foreign policy and the cooperation with MFA and Ministry of European Affairs".

As outlined in Chap. 4, the president chairs CSAT, the Supreme Council of National Defence. Its secretariat is located in the president's office, presidential advisers are strongly involved in shaping its work, and essentially CSAT is convened on the initiative of the president. Meetings are held roughly three times per year. The agenda of the Council can be quite broad, covering all types of matters related to external and internal security. The Council decides by consensus. The government is expected to implement the decisions taken by CSAT (Apostolache 2016). The president may also attend those government meetings "debating upon matters of national interest with regard to foreign policy, the defence of the country, ensurance of public order, and, at the Prime Minister's request, in other instances as well" (Article 87). But as explained in Chap. 4, such meetings have been held sparingly. This underlines the fact that most of foreign policy coordination occurs between the president and the foreign minister or the prime minister, with active administrative coordination between the president's office and the foreign ministry. Indeed, it can be argued that through such active contacts the foreign minister is more drawn to the president than to the prime minister.

Yet disputes do arrive, although not often. In 1991 President Iliescu and Prime Minister Roman disagreed about how Romania should respond to the coup in the Soviet Union, with Iliescu taking a more pro-Soviet Union stance whereas the government criticized strongly the coup in Moscow (Gherghina 2013: 264). In 1996 Iliescu essentially used CSAT to impose various measures related to security on the government. In June 2006, Prime Minister Popescu-Tăriceanu publicly announced the decision to withdraw the Romanian troops stationed in Afghanistan. President Băsescu criticized heavily such plans and the line of the president prevailed in CSAT (Gherghina and Miscoiu 2013: 676). In 2013 Băsescu accused Prime Minister Ponta of violating the 'cohabitation pact' between the two executives. Two of these incidents concerned foreign policy, with Băsescu noting that Ponta had adopted a different position than the president regarding the recognition of Kosovo's independence and how to react to the regime of Bashar Assad in Syria (Bucur 2013). In the spring of 2018 President Iohannis and Prime Minister Dăncilă disagreed about moving the Romanian embassy in Israel, with the president accusing the premier of avoiding contacts that are necessary for the successful implementation of foreign policy. In November 2018 Iohannis in turn asked for the Dăncilă government to resign, publicly questioning whether the cabinet was competent to handle the approaching EU presidency. The foreign ministry responded with an official statement, denying the presidential claims and stressing "the importance of handling with responsibility information that is not founded on concrete endeavours and which may affect the image of Romania, its credibility and its status at European level"[16] (Anghel 2018). As in domestic matters, tensions and behind-the-scenes disputes have been more common under cohabitation.

In Romania the government is responsible for the domestic coordination of EU affairs, with sectoral ministries coordinating positions with the permanent representation in Brussels. The government must inform the legislature about the agenda of the European Council summit, and the parliament then submits a non-bonding mandate on Romania's positions. The government must also inform the parliament afterward of decisions taken in the European Council (Gärtner et al. 2011; Tacea 2015).[17] Yet it is the president, as 'representative of the Romanian state', who travels to European Council summits. The prime minister can represent Romania only upon delegation by the president. Before the European Council, the president receives information from the foreign ministry and there is close coordination with the Romanian representative to the EU. After the summit the president does not have to report to the government or the parliament, although the presidential staff writes a report that is shared with the foreign ministry and the president usually holds a press conference. Beyond European Council meetings, CFSP/CSDP matters, and Treaty amendments, the presidents have so far normally not become involved in 'routine' EU matters, such as internal market legislation. This applies particularly to President Iohannis, whereas Băsescu displayed more activism in European affairs.

In fact, before Romania became an EU member, the president and the prime minister both claimed to represent Romania in the European Council (Gherghina and Miscoiu 2013: 677). In December 2006, Băsescu and Prime Minister Popescu-Tăriceanu traveled by separate planes to Brussels, and in April 2007 the two leaders had different strategies and agendas in the European Council. In the midst of the impeachment crisis in the summer of 2012 (see Chap. 5), a major conflict between Prime Minister Victor Ponta and President Băsescu broke out about the issue. Ponta, backed by the parliament, indicated his desire to represent the country in the European Council meeting scheduled for

28–29 June. Băsescu refused to accept this as the president had always led the Romanian delegation in the European Council sessions since Romania had joined the Union in 2007. On 27 June, a divided Constitutional Court ruled in Băsescu's favor, stating that as the president represents the country in foreign affairs, the prime minister could attend the European Council only on the basis of an express mandate from the president.[18] Ponta responded by accusing the constitutional judges of bias in favor of the president, with the prime minister then, in line with the court ruling, asking for an express mandate from Băsescu. The president denied such a mandate, but Ponta chose nonetheless to fly to Brussels as head of the Romanian delegation (Perju 2015). Afterward Ponta expressed his frustration repeatedly, referring to the lack of domestic accountability of the European Council meetings: "Băsescu is going to represent us at the European Council without even a sham consultation … Băsescu alone knows what is best: he does not waste his time with parliament, with the opposition or even with the government"[19] (Tacea 2015: 627). In December 2015 President Iohannis delegated Prime Minister Cioloş to represent Romania in the European Council, with Cioloş also attending the informal European Council meeting in March 2016 when Iohannis was on a state visit to Israel and Palestine (Bucur 2016). Apart from these episodes, the president has always represented Romania in the European Council.

The situation in Romania is thus both constitutionally and in practice more straightforward than in Lithuania or Finland. Leadership in external relations belongs to the president. The president is responsible for foreign and security policy, represents Romania in the European Council, and through CSAT is in charge of key security and defense policy decisions. The size of the presidential staff working on foreign and security policy questions is also considerably larger than in Lithuania and Finland, and this means that the presidential office is also actively involved in the preparatory work related to foreign policy decisions. At the same time we must remember that most of the day-to-day management of foreign affairs and EU issues is handled by the government—especially the foreign ministry but also the prime minister's office and the Ministry of Defence. This does cause occasional tensions and disputes, not least because it is the government that does the 'hard work' while the president receives the media coverage through signing international treaties and meeting foreign leaders.

6.4   Concluding Reflections: Consensus
but Potential for Disputes

Our analysis of decision-making in foreign and security policy and in EU affairs provides strong evidence in favor of our theoretical propositions formulated in Chap. 2. In all three countries intra-executive coordination is most developed and regular in external relations. This applies both to routine, day-to-day management of foreign affairs between the president and the government, including between the respective administrative staff, and to high-level decisions taken in security policy councils—the Ministerial Committee on Foreign and Security Policy in Finland, the State Defence Council in Lithuania, and CSAT in Romania. In all three countries the goal is to achieve consensus, to speak with one voice vis-à-vis other countries and in international organizations. For the most part this goal is also achieved. Prime ministers and presidents may engage in bitter quarrels about domestic matters, but in foreign and security policy they behave for the most part like 'statesmen', accepting compromises in the name of national interest.

Yet foreign and security policy and EU affairs are not exempt from intra-executive power struggles. In the preceding analysis we paid particular attention to the issue of who represents the country in the European Council, the main decision-making organ of the EU. Following the Lisbon Treaty, each member state is represented in the European Council either by the prime minister or by the president. In Finland the dispute ended in favor of the prime minister, with essentially all political parties and the Eduskunta supportive of the constitutional amendment which specifically regulates that the prime minister represents Finland in the European Council. The Finnish president is essentially prohibited from attending any EU meetings, including those related to CFSP/CSDP matters. In Lithuania and Romania, on the other hand, the constitution leaves room for interpretation, but in both countries it is the president who attends the summits of the European Council. From the perspective of accountability and domestic coordination of EU matters this is surely not ideal, given that the president does not have to report to the legislature either before or after the European Council meetings and as the preparatory work ahead of European Council meetings is carried out by the government. However, the president at the same time does have a legitimate claim to become involved at least in those EU decisions that are related to national foreign and security policies. National foreign policies are increasingly influenced by and linked to EU, and hence the foreign policy powers of the presidents are directly linked to the development of CFSP/CSDP. It hence appears that in semi-presidential systems domestic strains will be the more or less inevitable outcome when the formal rules vest the direction of foreign and/or EU policy conjointly in the president and the government (Raunio 2012).

Presidents are expected to stay 'above' party politics, looking after the interests of the entire country and, as the heads of armed forces, also ultimately responsible for the security and territorial integrity of the country. Hence it is quite logical that the respective office-holders are often seen as guarantors of national survival, with the public expecting them to stand firm and to show resolute leadership in times of trouble. This can also facilitate presidential power grabs. In line with the securitization thesis put forward in Chap. 2, the presidents have benefited from perceived external threats. This was most prominent in Lithuania, where President Grybauskaitė established her authority in defense policy following Russian invasion of Ukraine in 2014. In a similar way, President Niinistö in Finland took an active role in security policy, especially in bilateral Russian relations. In both cases such assertive presidential behavior was seemingly appreciated by the electorates.

NOTES

1. Perustuslakivaliokunnan mietintö 10/1998 (PeVM 10/1998 vp—HE 1/1998 vp). Hallituksen esitys uudeksi Suomen Hallitusmuodoksi, 26; see also Hallituksen esitys Eduskunnalle uudeksi Suomen Hallitusmuodoksi (HE 1/1998 vp): 146.
2. According to the Venice Commission this was foreseen by the drafters of constitution: "In defining the area of governmental primacy by reference to an entity, the EU, whose competence is continually shifting/expanding, the framers of the Finnish Constitution have deliberately provided for a growing area of primary governmental competence in foreign policy. The growth of common positions and strategies in the EU common foreign and security policy (CFSP), e.g. as regards what has traditionally been a crucially important part of Finnish foreign policy, its relationship with Russia, means that issues previously regarded as purely bilateral will now be regarded, depending on the circumstances, as partially, largely, or wholly, within the Government's primacy." Venice Commission, 'Opinion on the Constitution of Finland', Opinion No. 420/2007, Strasbourg, 7 April 2008.
3. Arto Astikainen, Presidentti ei voi olla reservissä, *Helsingin Sanomat*, 24 December 2003.

4. In May 2010 the government appointed, against the views of the president, the Finnish delegation to the EU-LAC (Latin America and Caribbean) summit. Hallitus otti loputkin EU-asioista itselleen, *Helsingin Sanomat*, 8 May 2010.

5. The Sipilä cabinet has a specific ministerial working group on Russia that brings together the president and those cabinet ministers interested in participating in its work.

6. HE 60/2010, Hallituksen esitys Eduskunnalle laiksi Suomen perustuslain muuttamisesta.

7. During her 12 years in office, President Halonen made 295 visits abroad (144 in her first term and 151 in the second term). During his first term Niinistö made 85 trips abroad (Mörttinen and Nurmi 2018: 184–185, 319–323).

8. President Niinistö remarked in an interview about co-leadership that "the constitution explicitly states that the President of the Republic directs … in co-operation. I always pause in the middle of the sentence." *Ylen Ykkösaamu*, 28 May 2016.

9. Mika Kari, a Social Democratic MP and the vice-chair of the Defence Committee in the Eduskunta, had wished that the government would allocate substantially more resources to the president's office, particularly in light of the more turbulent and fast-paced developments in international politics. Emphasizing the contacts with the foreign ministry, President Niinistö disagreed, stating his office does not need more resources. Mika Koskinen, Erikoishaastattelu: Presidentti Niinistö Sipilän roolista ulkopolitiikassa: "Aktiivisempi kuin yksikään muu pääministeri aikanani", *Iltalehti*, 19 August 2018, https://www.iltalehti.fi/politiikka/a/201808192201145268

10. As President Niinistö has repeatedly emphasized, in such situations the discussions in the European Council may deal with matters that fall under the co-leadership in foreign policy as regulated by Section 93 of the constitution. According to Niinistö there have been phone calls between him and the prime minister during the European Council dinners on two occasions, when the informal talks ventured into areas falling under the jurisdiction of the president. Ari Hakahuhta, Analyysi: Presidentti hillitsee jo puheita myyttisestä Putin-suhteesta—Niinistön asema ulkopolitiikan johtajana vahva. *Yle*, 29 August 2018, https://yle.fi/uutiset/3-10370652

11. The Law Supplementing the Constitution of the Republic of Lithuania with the Constitutional Act "On Membership of the Republic of Lithuania in the European Union" and Supplementing Article 150 of the Constitution of the Republic of Lithuania (No. IX-2343) of 13 July 2004, Valstybės žinios (Official Gazette), 2004, No. 111-4123.

12. The discontinuation of the Council may have stemmed from the plan of President Paksas to use the body for coordinating EU policy as well. The role of the Council was seen as limited and there were also concerns about its constitutional status.

13. In addition, new legislative changes were introduced which strengthen the powers of the president during times of war (Šlekys 2018).

14. Prior to EU membership in 2003, President Paksas demanded a major role for the president and his office in the domestic coordination of European affairs. As the impeachment of Paksas coincided with joining the EU and the design of the national EU coordination system, the role of the president ended up being quite limited. Also the president's office does not have sufficient resources for the daily management of EU issues (Maniokas and Vilpišauskas 2010: 22; Vilpišauskas 2015: 567).

15. Before President Grybauskaité enforced the resignation of Vygaudas Ušackas in early 2010, the foreign minister and the president did not communicate in person for several months (Krupavičius 2013: 228–229).

16. Ministry of Foreign Affairs, press release, 13 November 2018, https://www.mae.ro/en/node/47431

17. Hence, as in Lithuania, this undermines parliamentary accountability in EU affairs and especially regarding European Council meetings. Interestingly, in the midst of the conflict between Prime Minister Ponta and Băsescu about who represents Romania in the European Council, the parliament organized a special extraordinary plenary meeting of the two chambers after the European Council of 28–29 June 2012, with Ponta presenting a report on the summit. At the same time the parliament tried to adopt new legal provisions that would have strengthened the domestic accountability of the European Council, and particularly the participation rights of the legislature, but the law had to be modified as the Constitutional Court ruled that such provisions were unconstitutional. According to the original law, Romania could have been represented in the European Council either by the president or by the prime minister, and if the two leaders disagreed about who attends the summit, the parliament would have decided who leads the Romanian delegation to the European Council (Tacea 2015: 619, 626–627).

18. Decision no. 683/27 June 2012; http://www.ccr.ro/files/products/D0683_12.pdf

19. The blog of Prime Minister Ponta: http://blogponta.wordpress.com/2011/12/08/romania-cainele-surd-la-vanatoarea-europeana/

BIBLIOGRAPHY

Anghel, V. (2018, November 20). Romania – The President's 'Breaking Bad': When Does Negative Campaigning Work? *Presidential Power* blog. http://presidential-power.com/?p=8955

Apostolache, M. C. (2016). The Prime Minister and the Supreme Council of National Defence. *Journal of Law and Administrative Sciences, 6,* 45–57.

Bucur, C. (2013, October 18). Romania – Cohabitation. *Presidential Power* blog. http://presidential-power.com/?p=190

Bucur, C. (2016, March 16). Romania – President Iohannis' Contested Performance and a Brief Assessment of His Exercise of Constitutional Powers. *Presidential Power* blog. http://presidential-power.com/?p=4614

Gärtner, L., Hörner, J., & Obholzer, L. (2011). National Coordination of EU Policy: A Comparative Study of the Twelve "New" Member States. *Journal of Contemporary European Research, 7*(1), 77–100.

Gherghina, S. (2013). Formal and Informal Powers in a Semi-Presidential Regime: The Case of Romania. In V. Hloušek et al. (Eds.), *Presidents Above Parties? Presidents in Central and Eastern Europe, Their Formal Competencies and Informal Power* (pp. 257–270). Brno: Masaryk University.

Gherghina, S., & Miscoiu, S. (2013). The Failure of Cohabitation: Explaining the 2007 and 2012 Institutional Crises in Romania. *East European Politics & Societies and Cultures, 27*(4), 668–684.

Hallberg, P., Martikainen, T., Nousiainen, J., & Tiikkainen, P. (2009). *Presidentin valta: hallitsijanvallan ja parlamentarismin välinen jännite Suomessa 1919–2009.* Helsinki: WSOY.

Hämäläinen, U. (2013). Niinistö mukautui yhteisjohtajaksi. In S. Tiihonen, M. Pohls, & J. Korppi-Tommola (Eds.), *Presidentti johtaa: Suomalaisen valtiojohtamisen pitkä linja* (pp. 279–300). Helsinki: Siltala.

Hovila, M. (2014). Tasavallan presidentti ja yhteistyökäytäntö ulkopolitiikassa – vuoden 2012 toimivallan uudistus. *Lakimies, 112*(3), 392–412.

Hyvärinen, A., & Raunio, T. (2014). Who Decides What EU Issues Ministers Talk About? Explaining Governmental EU Policy Co-ordination in Finland. *Journal of Common Market Studies, 52*(5), 1019–1034.

Krupavičius, A. (2013). Lithuania's President: A Formal and Informal Power. In V. Hloušek et al. (Eds.), *Presidents Above Parties? Presidents in Central and Eastern Europe, Their Formal Competencies and Informal Power* (pp. 205–232). Brno: Masaryk University.

Maniokas, K., & Vilpišauskas, R. (2010). *National Coordination of European Policy in Lithuania: Analysis of a Double Transformation* (Unpublished Paper).

Mörttinen, M., & Nurmi, L. (2018). *Sauli Niinistö: Mäntyniemen herra.* Helsinki: Into.

Niskanen, M. (2006). Onko sotilaallinen kriisinhallintalaki ulkopolitiikan johtamista vai EU-asia? *Lakimies, 104*(2), 244–256.

Niskanen, M. (2009). *Tasavallan presidentin ulko- ja turvallisuuspoliittinen päätösvalta Suomen valtiosäännössä.* Rovaniemi: Acta Universitatis Lapponiensis 170, Lapin yliopistokustannus.

Oikeusministeriö. (2002). *Selvitys perustuslakiuudistuksen toimeenpanosta. Perustuslain seurantatyöryhmän mietintö.* Helsinki: Oikeusministeriön työryhmämietintöjä 7.

Park, A. (2018a, July 11). Lithuania – President Grybauskaite in an Intra-institutional Tug of War. *Presidential Power* blog. http://presidential-power.com/?p=8427

Park, A. (2018b, April 11). Lithuania – President Grybauskaite on an Extended "Vacation"? *Presidential Power blog.* http://presidential-power.com/?p=7943

Perju, V. (2015). The Romanian Double Executive and the 2012 Constitutional Crisis. *International Journal of Constitutional Law, 13*(1), 246–278.

Raunio, T. (2008). Parlamentaarinen vastuu ulkopolitiikkaan: Suomen ulkopolitiikan johtajuus uuden perustuslain aikana. *Politiikka, 50*(4), 250–265.

Raunio, T. (2012). Semi-Presidentialism and European Integration: Lessons from Finland for Constitutional Design. *Journal of European Public Policy, 19*(4), 567–584.

Raunio, T. (2016). Refusing to Be Sidelined: The Engagement of the Finnish Eduskunta in Foreign Affairs. *Scandinavian Political Studies, 39*(4), 312–332.

Raunio, T. (2018). Parliament as an Arena for Politicisation: The Finnish Eduskunta and Crisis Management Operations. *The British Journal of Politics and International Relations, 20*(1), 158–174.

Šlekys, D. (2018, August 22–25). *Defence Politics and Reshaping of the Lithuanian Semi-Presidential Regime.* Paper presented at the ECPR General Conference, Hamburg.

Tacea, A. (2015). The Slow Adaptation of a New Member State: The Romanian Parliament and European Integration. In C. Hefftler, C. Neuhold, O. Rozenberg, & J. Smith (Eds.), *The Palgrave Handbook of National Parliaments and the European Union* (pp. 613–631). Basingstoke: Palgrave Macmillan.

Tiilikainen, T. (2003). Suomen ulkopoliittinen johtamisjärjestelmä uuden perustuslain mukaan. *Politiikka, 45*(3), 212–222.

Vilpišauskas, R. (2015). Parliamentary Scrutiny of EU Affairs in Lithuania: The Dog That Rarely Barks. In C. Hefftler, C. Neuhold, O. Rozenberg, & J. Smith (Eds.), *The Palgrave Handbook of National Parliaments and the European Union* (pp. 563–577). Basingstoke: Palgrave Macmillan.

Yli-Huttula, T. (2018). *Presidentti ja porvarivalta: Ristiriitoja ja yhteistoimintaa tasavallan sisäpiirissä.* Helsinki: Otava.

CHAPTER 7

Conclusions

Semi-presidential regimes are vulnerable to conflicts between presidents and prime ministers. Previous research has offered strong evidence of such intra-executive disputes and of the causal mechanisms behind the conflicts. Periods of cohabitation, where the two leaders represent opposing political camps, tend to result in more adversarial relations between the president and the prime minister. Research also indicates that stronger presidential prerogatives correlate with the frequency or level of intra-executive conflicts. Many intra-executive conflicts are essentially struggles for power and influence. Executive disputes over policy, appointments, dismissals, representation, and constitutional prerogatives are hence logical expressions of the institutional competition embedded into the dual leadership structure of semi-presidentialism. Apparently intra-executive conflict has not led to any regime breakdowns in Europe. One may even contend that periods of intense conflict between institutional actors is a normal and healthy sign of any democracy and especially in young political systems. Yet, the repeated political crises in Romania show how intra-executive conflict can cause negative effects on political stability and system legitimacy. Hence it is not surprising that much of the literature has treated semi-presidentialism with notable suspicion.

This strand of research is highly important and has generated a lot of information that should also benefit real-world processes of constitutional reform. However, the purpose of our book has been to go beyond

© The Author(s) 2020
T. Raunio, T. Sedelius, *Semi-Presidential Policy-Making in Europe*,
Palgrave Studies in Presidential Politics,
https://doi.org/10.1007/978-3-030-16431-7_7

cohabitation and constitutional powers and to dig deeper into the relations between the two executives. We believe that presidential ambitions
and behavior can only be uncovered by research designs that also reach
'behind the scenes'. This means talking to people who know how the
president operates and how intra-executive coordination really functions.
We have specifically underlined the role of coordination mechanisms,
arguing that such mechanisms can have a strong, independent effect on
the relations between the president and the prime minister and thereby
more broadly on national policy-making. Our basic premise was fairly
straightforward: the less there is formal, regular coordination between
the two leaders, the more there is space for presidential activism. Formal
coordination mechanisms in a sense tame or constrain presidents—and
should overall contribute to smoother intra-executive relations.

This concluding chapter reflects on our findings and suggests avenues
for further research. Explaining how our findings advance scholarly understanding of presidents and intra-executive relations, we highlight the need
for research designs that pay closer attention to informal avenues of political influence. We finish the chapter with a critical discussion on the role of
presidents in modern democracies. Are presidents unruly trouble-makers,
a danger to stable governance, or much-needed guardians of national
interest above party-political squabbles?

7.1   Informal Avenues and Political Leadership

When deciding on our case selection, we wanted to compare countries
that have sufficiently similar constitutional regimes but display variation
regarding the socio-economic context and the dynamics of party politics
(Chap. 3). The presidents of Finland, Lithuania, and Romania enjoy
broadly comparable constitutional prerogatives, although the Finnish
presidency is vested with somewhat weaker powers. In all three countries
foreign policy is either led (Lithuania, Romania) or co-led by the president
(Finland). However, the difference lies not so much in constitutional rules
as in actual practices. Finland is an old democracy known for its political
stability and low level of corruption. The constitutional reform process
that culminated in the new unified constitution of 2000 was an orderly,
calm process based on broad party-political consensus. Lithuania and
Romania, in turn, are much younger democracies that needed to adopt
new constitutions in the heated circumstances of the early 1990s. Their
party systems tend to be less stable, with political parties often being vehi-
cles for the personal ambitions of individual politicians. Both countries,

particularly Romania, have also had serious problems with corruption. Not very surprisingly, Finns tend to trust their political institutions whereas Lithuanians and Romanians do not.

Our main findings—summarized in Table 7.1—need to be understood in the context of these rather fundamental societal differences. Finland is a country full of regulations, and hence the politicians and legal experts responsible for amending the constitution opted for formal coordination instruments that essentially force the president and the prime minister to cooperate regularly. The Finnish president chairs the Ministerial Committee on Foreign and Security Policy and meets both the prime minister and the foreign minister on an almost weekly basis. But perhaps even more important is the legacy of Urho Kekkonen, who ruled the land with an iron hand for quarter of a century from 1956 to 1981. There was a shared understanding among the political elites that the balance of power had shifted too far in favor of the president. There was thus the political will to significantly reduce the powers of the president, but also a recognition of the need to bind the president to governmental decision-making. In Finland it is still 30 years later perceived inappropriate for the president to become involved in matters falling under the jurisdiction of the cabinet and the Eduskunta. This applies particularly to government formation, as one of the key factors contributing to the position of Kekkonen was his ability to basically dominate government formation processes, cherry-picking prime ministers and vetoing ministerial candidates and even the inclusion of whole parties in cabinets. However, whether such collective understanding prevails in the future remains to be seen, especially when considering the popularity of Finnish presidents.

In Lithuania and Romania, on the other hand, it is certainly both legitimate and appropriate for the president to interfere in matters that constitutionally belong to the competence of the government. The transition to democracy in the early 1990s provided a critical juncture in terms of institutional design. Both countries opted for a stronger presidency than in Finland and, more importantly, decided against specific rules about intra-executive coordination mechanisms. Neither country utilizes ministerial committees that would enable regular exchange between the president and the government, and even though the president meets the prime minister often, the frequency of such bilateral meetings is very much dependent on individual office-holders. Both countries also offer evidence of communication breakdowns, with the president or the prime minister simply refusing to talk to one another. Crucially, it is the president who

Table 7.1   Summary of main findings

	Finland	Lithuania	Romania
Formal presidential powers	Weak—limited to co-leading foreign policy	Medium—mainly limited to foreign policy	Medium—apart from leading foreign policy, the president is expected to mediate between political actors
Norms about president's position	Citizens support active and stronger presidential influence	Citizens support active and stronger presidential influence	Citizens support active and stronger presidential influence
		It is appropriate for the president to intervene in matters under the jurisdiction of the government	It is appropriate for the president to intervene in matters under the jurisdiction of the government
Level of intra-executive conflict	Low—rare incidents with limited implications	Medium—relatively infrequent but occasionally with major consequences (resignations of prime ministers, public confrontations)	High—frequent and with severe implications (stalemate, impeachments, political crisis)
Level of intra-executive coordination	High—established and institutionalized, bilateral meetings, ministerial committee	Medium—non-institutionalized and office-holder dependent; still fairly effective and routines do exist	Weak—ad hoc and very much office-holder dependent
Level of coordination in foreign and security policy	High—isolated and inconsequential disagreements between the executives	High—isolated disagreements between the executives	High—infrequent disagreements between the executives
President's relationship with political parties	Presidents are above and detached from the parties	Presidents are detached from the parties, but utilize party links (two of the three presidents were elected as independent candidates)	Presidents are actively involved in the work of their parties and even campaign for them in elections

(*continued*)

Table 7.1 (continued)

	Finland	Lithuania	Romania
Administrative resources of presidential office	Minimal staff and limited budget	Small staff and limited budget; a high share of advisors work in policy areas falling under the competence of the government	Medium-sized staff and budget; a high share of advisors work in policy areas falling under the competence of the government
Presidential strategies during intra-executive conflict	Problem-solving behind the scenes	Influencing the formation and termination of governments	Influencing the formation and termination of governments
	Occasional public critique of the government	Going public— occasional strong criticism of the government, including in matters falling under the competence of the cabinet	Going public— repeated attacks on the government, including in matters falling under the competence of the cabinet
		Legislative vetoes	Legislative vetoes
		Power grabs (notably in EU policy)	Stretching presidential prerogatives

holds the initiative regarding interaction with the prime minister or the government. The level and forms of intra-executive coordination are thus very much determined by the president. In line with our theoretical framework, this clearly empowers the president.

An interesting dimension is party politics, or the role of political parties in facilitating or hindering presidential influence. In all three countries the president as the head of state is not formally a member of any party, but here we see notable variation. Romanian presidents are quite openly involved in the work of their parties: the presidents have attended various party congresses, maintain in general close ties with their parties, and even campaigned in favor of their parties in parliamentary elections. In Lithuania such party ties are much weaker, although we must remember that two of the three presidents, Adamkus and Grybauskaitė, were elected into office as independent candidates. In Finland the non-involvement of presidents in party politics is strictly observed. Future research should examine more closely how presidents use their parties or friendly legislative majorities to achieve policy goals. The Lithuanian and Romanian examples illustrate how 'outsider' presidents, such as Constantinescu and Iohannis, have found it much more difficult to shape politics than incumbents who have long experience from party politics.

Our analysis indicates the buffet table of strategies available for presidents to wield influence. Apart from using their constitutional prerogatives, presidents make active use of informal channels: they meet with individual politicians, including party leaders, hold important public speeches that typically enjoy wide media coverage, and establish close links with various interest groups and citizens' associations. Again such activities are obviously not regulated by any laws. Previous research has very much focused on visible actions—presidential vetoes or the role of the president in forming and dissolving cabinets. These are clearly important dimensions that deserve to be examined, but maybe influential presidents do not need to veto bills or reject governments. Given favorable circumstances, not least a friendly prime minister and a legislative majority, presidents can achieve a lot without leaving any public trace of their actions. This is why we deliberately relied heavily on interviews with people in key positions—mainly ministers and top-ranking civil servants in the offices of the president and the prime minister. If we want to understand how individual presidents behave, one simply must talk to such informants and identify how presidents seek to influence politics.

An important and so far under-researched theme is the role of presidential staff. Most of the research on political advisors has focused either on political communication or on the various tasks advisors perform for their ministers. In Finland the size of the presidential office is very small, and hence the Finnish president is strongly dependent on the preparatory work carried out by the government. This applies also to foreign and security policy, an issue area where the president still has constitutional powers. In Lithuania and particularly in Romania the presidential palaces have generous staff levels, meaning that the presidents have, if required, the capacity to look into policy questions in much more detail and to prepare various political documents. A striking and perhaps also a surprising finding concerns the portfolios that the staff focus on. Most of the staff working for the Lithuanian and Romanian presidents deal with policy areas that fall under the competence of the government—economic policy, education, social and health affairs, culture, and so on. Importantly, these persons follow developments in the ministries and the legislature, maintain active links with interest groups and other shareholders, and in general try to generate support for the positions and initiatives of the president.

Again, uncovering the role of the staff is not possible without in-depth interviews. Future research on political leadership should therefore pay close attention to advisors and other staff, including of course also in the office of the prime minister.

Intra-executive coordination is most institutionalized and regular in foreign and security policy. Research on foreign policy has shown how countries throughout the world try to make sure that they 'speak with one voice' in external relations. This applies especially to security policy, where decision-makers often emphasize national unity, arguing that disagreement at home might jeopardize the advancement of national goals in international negotiations. Finland uses a specific ministerial committee in foreign and security policy that meets around twice a month and brings together the president, the prime minister, and other cabinet members. Lithuania and Romania utilize national security councils that meet less often but are convened to discuss various topical matters related to security policy. All of these bodies decide by consensus. While there have been some public disputes or disagreements between the president and the government in Finland, Lithuania, and Romania, normally the goal of speaking with one voice in foreign and security policy is achieved. There is routine, day-to-day administrative interaction between the presidential office and the foreign ministry, and in all three countries the president meets the foreign minister on a regular basis.

A potentially highly important development concerns the definition of foreign and security policy. In line with the 'securitization' thesis outlined in Chap. 2, a broader definition of security policy can bolster the position of the president. Here one must remember that in Finland, Lithuania, and Romania, the president is very much perceived as the guarantor of national security and even survival. Defense policy and the decisions about armed forces are in all three countries normally handled by the government and specifically the Ministry of Defence, but following the annexation of Crimea by Russia and the start of the war in Ukraine in 2014, President Grybauskaitė became suddenly interested in defense issues and was the decisive force in increasing the size of the defense budget and in reintroducing conscription. Also in Finland the aggressive foreign policy of Russia has brought security questions to the fore, with President Niinistö adopting a highly visible role in the debates and maintaining active links with the Russian president and other foreign leaders. Obviously many issues falling under the jurisdiction of the government from energy policy to the treatment of refugees are linked to security policy, and hence open the door for potential presidential 'power grabs'.

Representation in the European Council has offered political drama in all three countries. After the Lisbon Treaty entered into force, each country is represented in the European Council either by its prime minister or the head of state. The new constitutional amendment from 2012 explicitly states that the prime minister represents Finland in the summits. Before that Finland was known for its policy of 'two plates', with both the president and the prime minister often traveling to the summits together. The Eduskunta had expressed serious concerns about lack of political accountability, as the prime minister must report to the parliament and its EU committee about the summits whereas the president has no similar obligations. Now the situation is thus very clear, with the government representing Finland in all EU meetings, including, for example, also more informal summits between the EU and countries or regions outside the Union.

The Lithuanian and Romanian constitutions are in turn silent about representation in the European Council, and in general do not say very much about how European matters are handled domestically. However, the constitutions of both countries do stipulate that foreign policy is led by the president, with the president thus being the main representative of the state in external relations. In Lithuania the government is responsible for the routine management of EU affairs, but President Adamkus nonetheless attended certain European Council meetings. Grybauskaitė in turn has monopolized representation in the summits, and this practice has not been seriously questioned, not even by the Seimas. Grybauskaitė essentially benefited from the weakness of the Kubilius cabinet which needed presidential support for its austerity measures. In Romania the president has traveled to the summits, and following the major dispute between Prime Minister Ponta and President Băsescu in 2012, the Constitutional Court ruled that the president represents Romania in the European Council. Again it is the legislature that loses control, as the president is not accountable to the parliament. Hence the Lithuanian and Romanian MPs only learn about the European Council meetings from second-hand sources. Our analysis also shows how Lithuanian and Romanian presidents have influenced other EU issues and have specific staff that focus on European matters. Existing studies of domestic coordination of European matters have until now mainly neglected the potential role of the president, but clearly future studies of semi-presidential EU member states must also examine whether and how the president is involved in European policy.

In line with institutional theory, our findings illustrate path dependency and the stickiness of initially adopted courses of action. While the first president of Lithuania following the transition to democracy, Algirdas Brazauskas, was very much considered a cautious statesman, he nonetheless established practices that have become the norm in Lithuanian politics. Brazauskas influenced government formation, forced a prime minister to resign, recruited staff that focus on issue areas falling under the jurisdiction of the government, and in general maintained active ties to various stakeholders. Presidents Adamkus and Grybauskaitė have displayed a more robust style of leadership, but have overall followed in the footsteps of Brazauskas. In Romania President Iliescu intervened actively in governmental affairs and did not hesitate to use his strong influence inside the Social Democratic Party for personal gains. President Băsescu behaved in a broadly similar fashion, adopting an assertive and even confrontational leadership style where links to his party were in a central role. Constantinescu and Iohannis had in turn different backgrounds with weaker ties to political parties, but also they attempted to influence both government formation and matters in the jurisdiction of the cabinet. Finland has had only two presidents under the new constitution, but it is clear that the broad party-political consensus achieved during the constitutional reform process has constrained Halonen and Niinistö.

Connecting our findings to the categories of informal institutions identified in Chap. 2, the types of presidential activism outlined in this book combine elements of accommodating and competing institutions. Most of the activism has undoubtedly sought to expand presidential influence while respecting the letter of the constitution. However, we have also identified clear examples of competing informal institutions, notably in Romania, where presidential behavior has clearly contradicted constitutional division of authority, not least through continuous interference in the work of governments. Bilateral meetings between the two leaders are in turn an excellent example of a complementary informal institution. Such meetings contribute to regime stability and efficient policy-making through facilitating trust and understanding between the president and the prime minister. In Finland these meetings have become a de facto formal institution. Also administrative coordination can be seen as a complementary institution, but as argued in this book, presidents can also use their staff for expanding their influence and for intervening in matters falling under the jurisdiction of the cabinet.

Overall, our findings are thus in line with our theoretical expectations. The more there is formal and regular coordination, the less space there is for presidential activism—and vice versa. At the same time we must underline the exploratory nature of our research. First, future research should be more systematic regarding both case selection and data. Our analysis covered only three countries, and thus the number of individual presidents in our dataset was small: two from Finland, three from Lithuania, and four from Romania. Secondly, we have so far in a sense only scratched the surface or focused on broader behavioral patterns. Various presidential activities—from public speeches, party links, to ties with various stakeholders—could be subjected to much closer examination and be linked to data on intra-executive conflicts or legislative vetoes. A third reservation concerns our approach. The overwhelming majority of research on semi-presidentialism has focused on presidents and their actions, giving much less space to the prime minister and the government. We have also emphasized how the presidents utilize various informal channels, but obviously one could also examine power-sharing more from the perspective of the government: what strategies do ministers use to influence the president and do the prime ministers or cabinet members criticize the president publicly? Here a logical example would be foreign and security policy, as in Lithuania and Romania it is directed by the president.

7.2   POPULAR AND DANGEROUS PRESIDENTS?

Existing research is not very favorable of presidents. In intra-executive conflicts the president is for the most part identified as the culprit: the president interferes in cabinet formation, uses hostile language toward the prime minister, wields legislative vetoes, or intervenes in policy questions under the competence of the cabinet. Certainly our findings also provide further evidence of the negative features associated with presidents and semi-presidential regimes. Most of the intra-executive conflicts or tensions in Finland, Lithuania, and Romania result from actions of the president. Here we need to remember a simple fact: presidents are almost without exception ambitious politicians who have strong preferences and political agendas. If the prime minister and the government do not agree with the president, conflicts are likely to emerge.

Interestingly, the Finnish, Lithuanian, and Romanian constitutions are often quite vague when it comes to delineating president's constitutional toolkit. This is of course a typical feature of semi-presidential countries—

but it is also a feature that can have serious political consequences, another well-established finding from previous research. In all three countries the government rules with the support of the legislature, but the president is given some kind of a role in cabinet formation. The Lithuanian and Romanian presidents could leave the selection of ministers entirely to the governing parties, but as the constitution leaves room for interpretation, the office-holders have not hesitated to intervene. In Finland the understanding is that the president should not interfere in any way in government formation, but the constitution certainly makes it perfectly possible for the president to influence both the selection of ministers and even the government program. The same applies to policy-making. The respective constitutions do explain the division of labor between the two executives, but obviously nothing prevents the president from commenting publicly on issues belonging to the competence of the government.

Here Romania is a particularly interesting case. When adopting its first democratic constitution, Romania was strongly influenced by the French version of semi-presidentialism. According to the French model, the president is above the parties and in that capacity responsible for the smooth functioning of the political system. According to Article 80(2) of the constitution, "the President of Romania shall guard the observance of the Constitution and the proper functioning of the public authorities. To this effect, he shall act as a mediator between the Powers in the State, as well as between the State and society." Our analysis and earlier literature on Romanian politics clearly show the challenges caused by this constitutional clause. In the impeachment cases against Băsescu, the president was accused of misusing his 'mediating' role. His political opponents argued that Băsescu had maintained too close ties to his own party and had unnecessarily interfered in the work of the government, the legislature, and even the courts. Drawing a clear line between mediation and interference is impossible, and in any case it is blatantly evident that it is considered appropriate for Romanian presidents to intervene in governmental affairs. Article 80(2) is in our opinion a highly problematic constitutional clause, and it has directly contributed to the high level of intra-executive conflicts found in Romania.

But herein lies a broader dilemma: should the presidents simply not use their constitutional prerogatives? This is of course perfectly possible, as studies of various semi-presidential regimes have shown. Even when it comes to leading foreign policy, presidents could effectively delegate leadership and representation of the country to the government. As we explained above, this is unlikely to happen considering the backgrounds and political ambitions of the incumbents. Presidents also need to decide what to do while in office. The prime minister, other cabinet members, and even parliamentarians have their calendars full of various meetings and other events. Particularly premiers and other key ministers are burdened with long days and hectic schedules. The calendar of the president, on the other hand, is far less busy. Routine duties, for example those relating to appointments, take at most a few hours per week. This is another advantage of the president—the incumbent can choose what kinds of activities to pursue, what events to attend, and when to become involved in politics. The prime minister enjoys no such luxury. The president can observe developments and choose the moments of intervention, and our analysis as well as previous research demonstrates that such interventions are more likely under cohabitation or when the government finds itself for some reason in trouble.

Political culture and the broader socio-economic context need to be taken into account. In Finland the presidents do not criticize the prime minister and the cabinet publicly. Disagreements do occur, but they are mainly handled behind the scenes without public conflicts. In Lithuania and Romania the situation is completely different. Presidents have adopted even quite confrontational stances, unleashing harsh attacks on the government. In many instances such public grandstanding has taken place in official, ceremonial duties—for example, when addressing the legislature. The presidents have questioned the competence and legitimacy of the government and have requested that the prime minister resigns. And the presidents have also emerged victorious from most of these public battles.

The presidents are as a standard rule considerably more popular than prime ministers and other party politicians. Hence it is not surprising that several office-holders in Lithuania and Romania have distanced themselves from the dirty waters of party politics, using quite strong populist, anti-party, or even anti-politics discourse. This is somewhat more understandable in Romania, where the anti-corruption agendas of the presidents have clearly resonated with the public mood. Overall, evidence from all three countries indicates that people expect solid leadership, with the presidents keeping the house in order. Romanian political and administrative elites may not have liked the abrasive style of President Băsescu, but it certainly did not harm his popularity ratings. Lithuanians also seem to appreciate the robust leadership shown by 'iron lady' Grybauskaitė.

Power-sharing between the president and the prime minister can provide much-needed checks and balances to the political system. In the context of serious societal turmoil, presidents can bring order and stability with their speeches, legislative vetoes, or other measures. Yet presidential powers and activism are a slippery slope, and therein lies the danger of accumulation of power in the hands of the president. The combination of direct elections and strong popularity works in favor of the president, especially in the personality-centered political cultures found in Central and Eastern European regimes. In Romania there have been attempts to decrease the constitutional prerogatives of the president, exactly because of the accumulation of power in the presidency and the strongly personalized political culture it embodies. The advantage of formal intra-executive coordination mechanisms is that they constrain both sides—the president and the prime minister. When the two executives meet on a regular basis and when there are formal rules structuring joint decision-making, presidents and prime ministers are simply much closer to one another. This facilitates trust and understanding between the leaders and reduces the scope for presidential activism. Such intra-executive coordination mechanisms need not be subject to constitutional regulation. They can be introduced by laws or decrees, but as we have argued in this book, presidents may have good reasons to prefer less regulation and more ad hoc practices.

Equally important are sufficiently clear constitutional rules. Most of the intra-executive conflicts are related to constitutional passages that open the door for presidential influence. This applies best to government formation, where the Lithuanian and Romanian presidents have benefited from vague constitutional clauses. The Lithuanian and Romanian constitutions do not explicitly state which leader represents the country in the European Council: in both countries the president attends the summits even though the government is responsible for the domestic management of EU affairs. And the 'mediating' role assigned to the Romanian president has definitely contributed to the high frequency and intensity of intra-executive conflict. Finally, we must emphasize that we are not arguing that politics in Finland, Lithuania, and Romania would be determined by the president. Winning presidential elections may well be the 'big prize' in national politics, but even in Lithuania and Romania it is the prime minister and the government that run the country and are the dominant executives in normal domestic and European matters. Yet we have shown how the real-world influence of presidents often exceeds their formal constitutional prerogatives, with presidents using various informal avenues of influence to shape politics.

Index[1]

A

Accommodating institutions, 23, 40
Adamkus, Valdas, 82, 85, 99, 101,
102, 104–107, 120, 139, 155,
158, 159
Administrative coordination, 79, 80,
87, 142
Agenda power, 28
Agenda setting, 12, 20, 36, 115
Aho, Esko, 61
Ahtisaari, Martti, 132
Austria, 47, 50

B

Băsescu, Traian, 58, 65, 66, 83, 86,
108–113, 115–118, 141–144,
158, 159, 161, 162
Belarus, 46, 47, 50, 52
Bilateral meetings, 2, 38, 79, 80, 84,
102, 130, 153, 159
Blue Reform (Finland), 95

Boc, Emil, 83, 110, 111
Brazauskas, Algirdas, 82, 85, 89,
99–102, 104–107, 159
Bulgaria, 50
Butkevičius, Algirdas, 103, 105,
138

C

Ceaușescu, Nicolae, 56, 74n2
Central and Eastern Europe, v, 29, 49,
120, 163
Central Europe, 8, 30, 47, 48, 68
Centre Party of Finland (KESK)
(Finland), 95
Christian Democratic-National
Peasants Party (PNT-CD)
(Romania), 113
Cioloș, Dacian, 113, 114, 144
Ciorbea, Victor, 83, 113
Civil servants, 6, 10, 13, 25, 39–40,
79, 82, 84, 87, 156

---

[1] Note: Page numbers followed by 'n' refer to notes.

© The Author(s) 2020   165
T. Raunio, T. Sedelius, *Semi-Presidential Policy-Making in Europe*,
Palgrave Studies in Presidential Politics,
https://doi.org/10.1007/978-3-030-16431-7

Cohabitation, 5, 9, 11, 12, 28–29, 36, 45, 58–66, 72, 74n1, 82, 95, 99, 101, 107–110, 115, 117, 118, 120, 134, 141, 143, 151, 152, 162
Common Foreign and Security Policy (CFSP)/Common Security and Defence Policy (CSDP), 34, 39, 82, 128, 130–134, 143, 145, 146
Competing institutions, 24, 40, 159
Complementary institutions, 23, 159
Constantinescu, Emil, 65, 83, 86, 112, 113, 115, 156, 159
Constitutional Court, 56, 64, 66, 105, 109, 111, 116–118, 158
Coordination instruments, 33, 34, 36, 37, 140, 153
Coordination mechanisms, v, 9, 12, 13, 20, 27, 34–40, 72, 73, 79–89, 93, 121, 140, 152, 153, 163
Corruption, 9, 11, 23, 24, 27, 51, 72, 104, 109, 113, 114, 152, 153
Critical junctures, 21, 25, 47, 87, 94, 153
Croatia, 47, 50
Czech Republic, 50, 67, 68, 71

D
Dăncilă, Vasilica, 83, 113, 114, 142, 143
Decision-making, 6–8, 12, 13, 23, 24, 26, 29, 30, 36, 38, 40, 57, 80, 87, 88, 93, 101, 103, 118, 127–146, 163
Decree power, 54, 56
Defense policy, 32, 34, 85–88, 127, 130, 135–138, 140, 144, 146, 157
Democratic Alliance of Hungarians (UDMR) (Romania), 110

Democratic Convention (Romania), 65, 112
Democratic Liberal Party (PDL) (Romania), 110, 117
Democratic Party (PD) (Romania), 109, 110, 116, 117
Divided government, 1, 6

E
Eastern Europe, 5, 47, 60
Eduskunta, 48, 94, 95, 97–99, 119, 128–130, 132, 133, 135, 145, 153, 158
European Council, 13, 31, 34, 63, 64, 88, 96, 101, 111, 112, 127, 128, 132–135, 138–140, 143–145, 158, 163
European Union (EU), 4, 31
European Union (EU) affairs, 13, 20, 30, 33, 34, 39, 70, 79, 97, 101, 119, 121, 127–146, 158, 163
Executive conflict, 19, 30
Expert interviews, vi, 2, 6, 9–10, 36, 73

F
Farmers and Greens Union (LVZS) (Lithuania), 103, 104
Finland, vi, 2, 6–8, 10, 11, 13, 24, 45, 47, 48, 50–53, 55–58, 60, 64, 69–72, 80–88, 93–99, 104, 108, 116, 119, 120, 127–135, 141, 144–146, 152, 153, 155–163
Finns Party (Finland), 95
Focused comparison, v, 8, 45, 50, 74
Foreign affairs, 27, 31, 33, 39, 56, 65, 83, 86, 99, 100, 102, 104, 112, 113, 128, 129, 133, 134, 138, 141–145

Foreign policy, v, vi, 3, 6, 7, 12–14, 20, 30–34, 36, 39, 48, 55, 56, 79, 82, 84, 86, 87, 95, 99–101, 103, 106, 112, 115, 116, 128–136, 138–146, 152, 157, 158, 161
Formal institutions, 23–25, 38
France, 36, 47, 49, 50, 65, 108

G
Going public, 27, 29, 36, 40, 115, 116, 118
Grindeanu, Sorin, 66, 113, 114
Grybauskaitė, Dalia, 82, 99, 102–107, 136–140, 146, 155, 157–159, 162

H
Halonen, Tarja, 60, 83, 84, 96, 119, 130–132, 134, 159
Homeland Union-Christian Democrats (TS-LKD) (Lithuania), 100, 102

I
Iceland, 46, 47, 50
Iliescu, Ion, 9, 64, 65, 71, 74n2, 83, 86, 89, 108, 109, 113, 115, 116, 118, 142, 159
Impeachment, 9, 64, 66, 102, 109, 111, 112, 114, 117, 141, 143, 161
Informal institutions, 22–25, 28, 30, 38–40, 79, 80, 93, 159
Institutional coordination, vi, 2
Intra-executive conflict, 2, 5, 7, 8, 11, 12, 35, 36, 38, 45, 49, 58–65, 72, 73, 110, 115, 151, 160, 161, 163

Iohannis, Klaus, 65, 66, 83, 86, 108, 112–116, 142–144, 156, 159
Ireland, 46, 47, 50, 60
Isarescu, Constantin, 113

J
Joint committees/joint councils, 12, 38–39, 79, 85

K
Katainen, Jyrki, 61
Kekkonen, Urho, 57, 71, 88, 98, 119, 153
Kirkilas, Gediminas, 62
Kiviniemi, Mari, 61
Koivisto, Mauno, 57, 94
Kubilius, Andrius, 103, 139, 158

L
Labour Party of Lithuania (LDLP/ LDDP), 49, 100
Landsbergis, Vytautas, 49, 88
Liberal and Centre Union (LLS) (Lithuania), 102
Liberal Union of Lithuania (LLS), 104
Lipponen, Paavo, 83, 132
Lisbon Treaty, 63, 132, 133, 139, 145, 158
Lithuania, vi, 2, 45, 80–87, 93, 127, 152

M
Macedonia, 50
Ministerial Committee on Foreign and Security Policy (Finland), 80, 83–85, 93, 98, 119, 129, 130, 134, 145, 153
Moldova, 50, 140
Montenegro, 50

N

Nastase, Adrian, 109
National Coalition (KOK) (Finland),
    94–96
National Liberal Party (PNL)
    (Romania), 109, 113
National Salvation Front (NSF)
    (Romania), 49, 89, 108
National security, 32, 33, 39, 56, 79,
    86, 103, 107, 112, 115, 116,
    137, 140, 157
National security council, 39, 84, 130,
    157
NATO, *see* North Atlantic Treaty
    Organization
New Institutionalism, 5
Niinistö, Sauli, 84, 95–97, 99, 119,
    129, 130, 132, 134, 135, 157,
    159
North Atlantic Treaty Organization
    (NATO), 8, 31–33, 72, 82, 85,
    113, 136, 141

P

Paksas, Rolandas, 64, 99, 102, 104,
    106
Path dependency, 5, 20, 21, 26, 159
Poland, 50, 67, 68, 71
Policy
    coordination, 1, 2, 6, 8, 9, 13, 14,
        20–26, 33, 131, 136, 142
    gridlock, 21, 26
    influence, 26, 28, 156
Policy-making, vi, 2, 6–9, 12, 13, 19,
    26, 27, 30, 33, 64, 65, 89, 94,
    103, 152, 159
Political leadership, v, vi, 3, 6, 12, 20,
    30, 33, 152–160
Ponta, Victor, 58, 66, 111–114, 117,
    141–144, 158

Popescu-Tăriceanu, Calin, 66, 109,
    110, 142, 143
Popular Movement Party (PMP)
    (Romania), 117
Power-sharing, vi, 2, 3, 9, 13, 23, 24,
    30, 58, 64, 71, 160, 163
Premier-presidentialism, 4, 12, 46, 48,
    50, 52, 53
Presidential activism, 2, 9, 11, 12, 29,
    30, 34–36, 40, 64, 72, 73, 80,
    93, 94, 97, 105, 107, 108,
    118–121, 134, 152, 159, 160,
    163
Presidential administration, 6, 116
Presidentialism, 3, 4, 19, 24, 49
Presidentialization, 29, 40, 110
Presidential power, 1, 5, 11, 12, 28,
    45, 47, 52–60, 70–73, 88, 109,
    111, 119, 146, 163
President-parliamentarism, 4, 12, 45,
    46, 52
Public administration, v, vi, 3, 6, 12,
    20, 56, 141
Public opinion/public support/public
    trust, 12, 29, 36, 45, 66–72, 97,
    139

R

Rational choice, 21
Referendum, 66, 88, 111, 114
Roman, Petre, 9, 49, 64, 109,
    142
Romania, vi, 2, 7–10, 13, 45, 49–54,
    56, 58, 64, 66–68, 71–73,
    80–89, 93, 99, 108–120, 127,
    130, 131, 135, 141–145,
    151–153, 156–163
Russia, 31–33, 46, 47, 50, 52, 82, 84,
    85, 104, 109, 131, 132, 135,
    136, 140, 157

S

Sąjūdis (Lithuania), 49, 88

Securitization thesis, 138, 146, 157

Security policy, 7, 13, 20, 26, 31–33, 38, 39, 71, 84–88, 96, 98, 101, 103, 106, 119, 121, 127–131, 134, 138–140, 144–146, 156–158, 160

Seimas, 64, 85, 100–102, 104–108, 135, 137, 138, 141, 158

Semi-presidentialism, v, vi, 1–9, 11, 12, 14n1, 19, 20, 24–30, 36, 45–47, 52, 58, 65, 72–74, 107, 151, 160, 161

Serbia, 50

Sipilä, Juha, 95, 97, 134

Skvernelis, Saulius, 103, 105, 139, 140

Šleževičius, Adolfas, 104

Slovakia, 50

Slovenia, 46, 50

Social Democratic-Alliance of Liberals and Democrats (Romania), 114

Social Democratic Party of Finland (SDP) (Finland), 61

Social Democratic Party of Lithuania (LSDP), 61, 62

Social Democratic Party of Romania (PD/PDSR/PSD/PSDR), 66, 109, 110, 137, 159

Social Liberal Union (USL) (Romania), 112

Soviet Union, 4, 8, 57, 128, 142

Stankevičius, Laurynas, 104

State Defence Council (Lithuania), 85, 135–137, 145

Stubb, Alexander, 61

Substitutive institutions, 23, 24

Supreme Council of National Defence (CSAT) (Romania), 86, 141, 142, 144, 145

T

Tudose, Mihai, 113

U

Ukraine, 47, 50, 52, 58, 85, 132, 135, 136, 140, 146, 157

V

Vacaroiu, Nicolae, 83, 109

Vagnorius, Gediminas, 101, 104, 106

Vanhanen, Matti, 60

Vasile, Radu, 65, 113

Veto, 7, 8, 13, 28, 29, 34–36, 54, 57, 98, 105, 116, 120, 133, 153, 156, 160, 163

Printed by Printforce, the Netherlands